D0512128

Making Fresh Pasta

Making Fresh *Pasta*

DELICIOUS
HANDMADE,
HOMEMADE
RECIPES

ALIZA GREEN
WITH PHOTOGRAPHY
BY STEVE LEGATO

First published in the UK in 2012 by
Apple Press
74–77 White Lion Street
London N1 9PF
United Kingdom
www.QuartoKnows.com

ISBN-13: 978-1-84543-434-2

10 9 8 7 6 5

Design: Sandra Salamony
Photography: Steve Legato, except for page 41 by Aliza Green

Printed in China

I dedicate this book to the pasta artisans of the world,
who create delicious art with their hands daily.

CONTENTS

PART I: **THE BASICS**

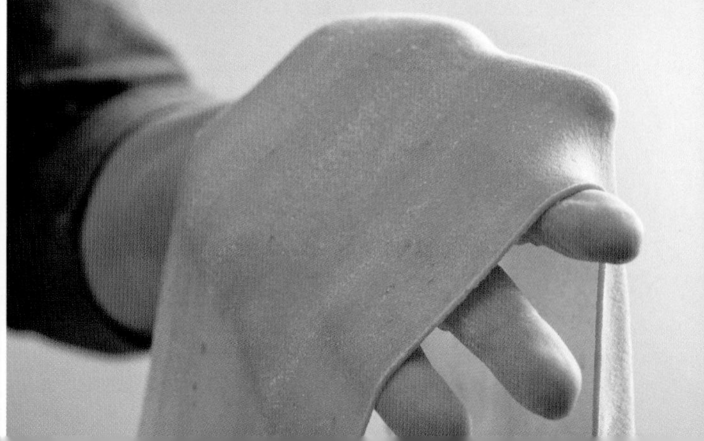

PART II: **THE PASTA**

CHAPTER FOUR:
DUMPLINGS 64

CHAPTER FIVE:
PASTA SHEETS 80

CHAPTER SIX:
MAKING CUT PASTA 94

CHAPTER SEVEN:
SPECIALTY HAND-FORMED PASTA 114

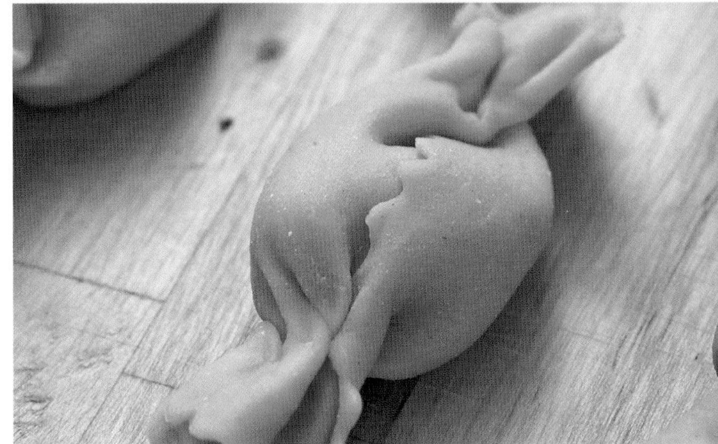

CHAPTER EIGHT:
STUFFED PASTA 134

FOREWORD

I FIRST MET ALIZA GREEN when she was working on a new edition of her book, *The Bean Bible*. A fellow *mangiafagioli* (bean eater - also a nickname for people from Tuscany, my home), she contacted me to learn more about the heirloom Tuscan beans that I import for my company, The Republic of Beans.

We hit it off immediately because we share a love of rustic, unpretentious food with strong roots in tradition and contemporary creativity. She understands cooking from both the heart and the intellect. As a lifelong food explorer, voracious reader, and accomplished self-taught chef, Aliza is flexible and curious, and she's a relentless researcher. I don't know many chefs who would spend five years studying Italian just to be able to cook more authentic food!

Aliza spent many years developing her pasta skills, preparing traditional and creative fresh pasta for customers in the restaurants where she established a well-deserved reputation as one of Philadelphia's top chefs, at a time when few thought of that city as a culinary centre. To research *Making Fresh Pasta* and hone her pasta techniques, she worked with chefs, artisan pasta makers, and home cooks in Italy and elsewhere.

One of my earliest memories is learning from my grandmother how to hand roll *tordelli*, a traditional pasta from my home town of Lucca. I can still practically do it in my sleep. Follow Aliza's detailed instructions, accompanied by Steve Legato's clear, attractive photographs, and even if you don't have an Italian grandmother, you can learn to make excellent hand rolled pasta for tagliolini, tortelli (another name for ravioli), and tortelloni. A personal favourite is pappardelle, the wide ribbon-shaped pasta that has been a Tuscan specialty for hundreds of years, always served with a slow-cooked, herb-scented meat or game ragù.

In Italy, we eat pasta as just one of five courses:

- **ANTIPASTI** (appetizers such as marinated vegetables, olives, thin-sliced cured meats - or pimzimonio or raw vegetables dipped in extra virgin olive oil)
- **PRIMI** (first course, pasta, soup, polenta, or risotto)
- **SECONDI** (meat course, not a gigantic steak)
- **CONTORNI** (side dishes, vegetables)
- **DOLCI** (sweets, not too much and not too sweet).

Because the meat is surrounded by other foods, we Tuscans, though meat is important to us, eat it in smaller portions. This was originally because of economics, but now we also consider environmental and health concerns. We don't drown our pasta in sauce, and we cook it so it is quite chewy, which is both more healthful and more fun.

I'm not a purist. I don't think everything has to be done the same way it was one hundred or two hundred years ago, with specific ingredients and presentation. If anything, it's the opposite. I love taking traditional dishes from Veneto, Puglia, even ancient Rome and translating them into something new. I like "free-range" cooking that takes inspirations from all periods and all of Italy. In *Making Artisan Pasta*, Aliza includes classic Italian recipes like tortellini from Bologna, ombrichelli from Orvieto, and corzetti from Genoa, as well as manti from Turkey, pierogi from Poland, and nouilles from Alsace so readers can learn and experiment freely.

Aliza teaches us why some flours yield dough that stretches easily and others yield dough that snaps back like a rubber band; why some flours yield meltingly tender pasta and others yield chewy pasta with a bite. She describes how the three main ingredients in fresh pasta dough - flour, eggs, and water - work, not just taste. If your potato gnocchi taste more like "potato bullets" (an old Italian name for gnocchi translates to this), through Aliza's techniques you'll succeed in making light, tender gnocchi anyone would be proud to serve. Perhaps you've wanted to try passatelli, garganelli, or cavatelli? Don't settle for mediocre industrial "fresh" pasta, and don't be intimidated by lack of experience. Follow Aliza's instructions and you're sure to succeed.

Aliza's pasta is a delicious combination of authentic and traditional, creative and seasonal hailing from many parts of the world. In *Making Artisan Pasta*, she makes the techniques easy to understand and recreate for home cooks working in home kitchens in the real world, though professionals will gain valuable knowledge from this book. Aliza's genuine love of pasta shines here, encouraging readers to try it for themselves and even learn to make the ultimate: their own hand-stretched pasta.

And, I even use Aliza's books to teach my staff about their star ingredients.

- CESARE CASELLA
Dean of the Italian Culinary Academy, New York City

INTRODUCTION

Ridged bronze pasta cutting wheel

MAKING YOUR OWN PASTA is a satisfying way to work with your hands to create something beautiful and delicious from ingredients that you choose. Handmade artisan pasta (especially hand-stretched dough) is full of character: silky, chewy texture; full, fresh flavour; and pure, bright colour. You can roll the dough to any thickness and cut it in any shape. For stuffed pasta, you can create your own fillings from top-quality ingredients, without preservatives - local and seasonal if you desire - and seasoned to your taste.

To make most of the pastas in this book, you'll need only a few well-made tools, reasonable kitchen skills, and some upper body strength. I share helpful tips from many years of experience, some of the pitfalls, and how to fix your mistakes. Remember: The project that doesn't work out teaches you the most.

Pasta is fun for all ages, too. Children love cranking out the sheets of dough, then using a ravioli plaque to fill their own ravioli. Adults love sampling new shapes, flavours, fillings, and sauces, and everyone can enjoy the many flavours, shapes, and textures of pasta. As with all simple foods such as bread and ice cream, the quality of ingredients, their proportion, technique, and combination is essential.

I had the privilege of learning to make fresh pasta from Marcella Hazan, who was responsible for introducing the cuisine of Bologna to the United States in the late 1970s, as well as by working with skilled pasta artisans from Southern and Northern Italy. Bologna is known as *La Grassa*, the fat, because of the copious amounts of eggs, aged cheese, and fine *salumeria* (cured meats) used there in the heart of Italy's fresh pasta belt. Back then, I spent time in the kitchens of several Bolognese restaurants where the pasta was made every day from deep red-orange eggs and ultra-silky 00 flour finely milled especially for pasta and hand-stretched into enormous sheets, thin and large as a tablecloth.

Over time, new frozen "fresh" pasta companies grew, so chefs no longer needed to make their own pasta. Soon, everyone was serving "homemade" ravioli, and it was no longer special. But there is no doubt that for each step you take away from the handmade product that is made fresh every day, something subtle but important is lost.

FANTE'S KITCHEN WARES SHOP

Virtually all the specialty tools used in this book came from Fante's, located in the heart of Philadelphia's historic Italian Market. In 1906 the Fante family, Italian immigrants, opened the shop where they sold furniture and tableware and installed kitchens. They began importing European pastry tools, and by the 1960s, Fante's had expanded its line and became rightly known as "the store that has everything." In 1981, the Fante family retired and ownership passed to the store's then–general manager, Mariella Giovannucci, and her two brothers, who are still at the store every day answering every possible question about every kitchen tool imaginable.

SAVING TIME, ENSURING QUALITY

There are some helpful timesavers available. These days, I no longer have to laboriously extract the small silvery-skinned ink sacs from fresh squid. Instead, I buy squid ink, which is imported from Spain, and use just a teaspoon or two to flavour and colour pasta dough. Although products such as powdered spinach and beets for colouring pasta are available, I prefer to cook and purée my own vegetables, though I often use prepared roasted peppers. The added flavour, texture, and brilliant colour of added vegetable purées make this pasta truly unique.

Making Artisan Pasta is about the satisfying pleasure of working with your hands, using simple tools and a wooden table to create traditional and creative flavours and shapes of fresh artisan pasta to share with family and friends. Although most of the techniques in this book come from Italy, I also explore pasta traditions from Poland (pierogi), Greece (trahana), France (nouilles), Japan (udon noodles), China (pot stickers), Eastern Europe (matzo balls), and Turkey (manti) - all delicious, creative variations on dough made from flour and liquid.

My wish is that you have a lot of fun learning these techniques and enjoy for many years the visceral and sensuous pleasures of artisan pasta making. I am always happy to hear from readers, so please send me a message using the Ask Aliza tab on my website, www.alizagreen.com, and I'll be sure to answer.

- ALIZA GREEN

Large square ravioli stamp

PART I:
THE BASICS

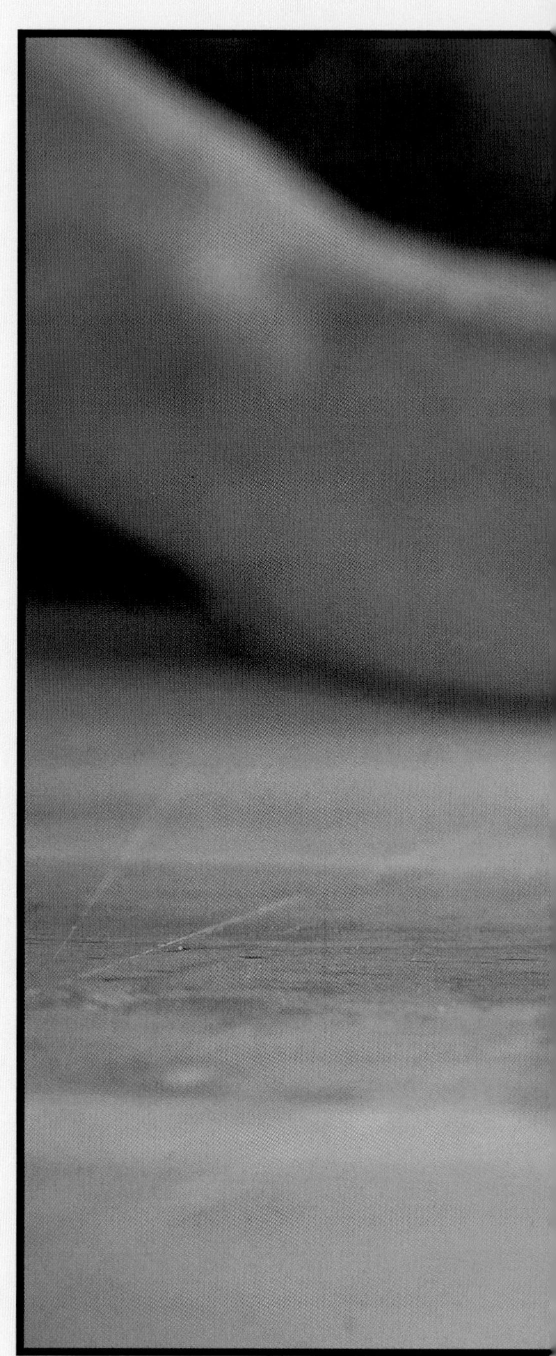

CHAPTER ONE

PASTA INGREDIENTS

IN THIS CHAPTER, you'll learn the techniques of making fresh pasta dough. Like bread, pasta is created from the most basic of ingredients - at its simplest just flour and water, though for handmade artisan pasta, the liquid is usually eggs. Wheat flour is the main ingredient and its quality, freshness, texture, and amount and type of gluten is critical. The better the flour, the better the pasta, and in this chapter I'll explain which to choose and why as well as what type of water is best, and how to choose eggs.

Below: Rye reginette - wide, flat ribbon pasta with pinked edges on both sides. This pasta shape dates from 1902 and originated in Naples, where it was created to celebrate the birth of Italy's "little queen," or _reginette_, Princess Mafalda. It is also known as Mafaldine.

In Northern Italy, fresh pasta dough is usually made from very finely ground soft, or winter, wheat, a variety of *Triticum aestivum*, which grows better in damp climates. This soft flour (*grano tenero* in Italian) is low in gluten proteins, yielding tender pasta suited to delicate sauces, its tenderness balanced by the additional protein structure provided by egg. Bread flour, another variety of *Triticum aestivum*, is not especially good for pasta as the type of gluten it contains is strong and elastic, perfect to contain air bubbles in bread dough but difficult to roll into thin sheets for pasta as it tends to spring back.

In Southern Italy, Sicily, and Sardinia, pasta is often made from higher-protein durum wheat, *Triticum durum*, which grows well in dry climates. Commercial dry pasta is almost always made from 100 percent durum because it dries without crumbling and holds intricate shapes well. Durum wheat contains strong gluten proteins for firm texture, but because its gluten is extensible rather than elastic, pasta dough made with durum rolls out more easily.

Rolling out red pepper pasta dough

China is the historical source of Asia's ancient and highly developed noodle and dumpling traditions. It is possible that stuffed dumplings traveled from Siberia and Central Asia to China. In China's north, soft wheat flour is more commonly used for noodles and dumpling wrappers while tender, translucent rice flour-based doughs are more common in the south especially for soup noodles, soup dumplings (wonton), and steamed dumplings (shu mai).

For many of the pastas in this book, I use a blend of flours - unbleached all-purpose flour, golden grainy durum semolina, and pale yellow durum flour - for chewy yet tender texture. However, you don't need to buy anything special as many pasta experts recommend using unbleached all-purpose flour. (All-purpose flour contains a moderate amount of protein and may be a combination of lower-protein pastry flour and higher-protein bread flour, or it may be simply milled from lower-protein soft wheat flour.) Freshly milled local artisanal flour and silky smooth Italian 00 flour yield pasta with excellent wheat flavour and supple, malleable texture. Some Italian artisan pasta makers prefer 0 flour, which is closer to unbleached all-purpose in texture and absorption qualities.

To make dough with whole wheat, buckwheat, spelt, cornmeal, rye, or other lower-protein flours, I mix them with higher protein unbleached all-purpose or Italian 00 flour. On their own, specialty flours yield mealy, crumbly dough because the rough fibres they contain tend to break gluten proteins. I avoid durum here because, combined with dark flours, it makes for an odd-coloured dough, especially if the liquid is egg.

For doughs containing vegetable purées such as spinach, winter squash, or roasted red peppers, I often use durum flour to increase protein content and because its nutty flavour and golden colour pairs well with vegetables. Other ingredients, including dried porcini mushrooms, chestnut flour, and saffron threads, call for their own combinations of flour and liquid: whole eggs, egg yolks, egg whites, water, or wine.

From left to right: **dark rye pasta, yellow cornmeal–chipotle, whole wheat, buckwheat, pasta flour blend (unbleached all-purpose wheat flour with durum and semolina), and cocoa**

Once you learn to make the Basic Egg Pasta Dough and get a feel for how it constantly evolves as it rests, as it's rolled out, and as it dries, you can expand your repertoire to making flavoured doughs. Try inky-black squid ink pasta perfect for cappellini and seafood-based liquidy sauces, chestnut flour and white wine dough used for the decorative stamped pasta coins from Genoa called corzetti, and smooth, chewy Umbrian red wine pasta that complements the region's hearty wild game, mushrooms, and truffles.

SELECTING INGREDIENTS

If you're going to take the time and effort to make your own pasta, start with the best ingredients, especially the most important ones: water, eggs, and flour. Luckily, even top-quality eggs and flour are relatively inexpensive and easy to find, while mineral-rich hard water from your tap is best for pasta dough. Experiment with different brands and types of flours to find your favourite. There is no right and wrong here: Some people prefer tender pasta made from soft wheat flour, others go for the chewy bite of pasta made from durum and semolina. Imported Italian 00 is silky, fine, and easy to roll out, and lately I've been making pasta with creamy, white Korean flour made from soft wheat.

WATER

Water, including the water in eggs, greatly influences the dough quality. (Bread dough may contain as much as 45 percent water in soft doughs such as ciabatta.) Hard water and sea salt contain minerals such as calcium and magnesium, which produce a firmer dough with a tighter gluten network than soft water. A pinch of salt, at most, is added to Italian pasta doughs, because it tends to harden them. To compensate, the resulting pasta is boiled in generously salted water to add flavour and help keep the pasta *al dente*, or toothsome. Even the temperature of the water is significant. For most recipes, tepid water is best to keep everything at room temperature so the liquid is more easily absorbed by the flour. However, some Asian noodle doughs, such as dumpling wrappers, are often made with hot or even boiling water to increase gluten elasticity.

PASTA AL DENTE

The preference for firm cooked pasta developed in eighteenth-century Naples, which became the centre of Italy's dried pasta production because its breezy climate was perfect for air-drying pasta, crucial before the invention of mechanical dryers. Earlier, pasta was cooked until quite soft, but when Neapolitan street vendors began selling pasta from carts, customers came to prefer pasta with chewy, substantial texture that was easier to eat with the hands, as was then the custom. By the nineteenth century, their taste for firm pasta had spread to the rest of Italy, though the term "al dente," meaning "to the tooth," didn't appear in the Italian language until after World War I.

We now know that the starch molecules in pasta are packed so tightly that only about half are digested rapidly as long as the pasta is kept firm and bouncy. So, pasta that is cooked al dente is easier to digest and more healthful.

HOW MUCH LIQUID PASTA DOUGH ABSORBS

Pasta dough contains 25 to 30 percent water depending on the type of flour used and the dryness of the ambient air. Each 12 ounces (350 g) of flour will absorb about 6 tablespoons (90 ml) water or 3 large eggs.

EGGS

Fresh pasta dough contains about 1 part egg to 2 parts flour by weight. The standard Italian proportion for handmade egg pasta is 1 medium egg (50 g) per 100 grams (3.5 ounces) of soft wheat flour. Most commonly, chicken eggs are used to make fresh pasta, though duck eggs are traditional for Venetian whole wheat bigoli, and giant goose eggs, sometimes found at farmers' markets, make very rich pasta dough. (One goose egg is the equivalent of a dozen hen's eggs!)

Eggs enhance the colour, richness, and smooth texture of pasta, especially the yolks, which may be used alone. Eggs also provide a second form of protein (along with gluten) that enhances dough structure and makes it easier to roll out thinly without tearing. Egg whites, which are high in protein and contain more water than the yolks, make for cohesive, firm pasta dough and prevent the loss of starch in the cooking water. They are occasionally used alone, as in red wine fettuccine (page 56).

In general, the thinner the eventual width of the pasta strip, the higher the proportion of egg yolks because of the strength and richness they add to the dough. Because All-Yolk Dough is so rich, it is best suited to Tagliolini (page 106) and Tortellini (page 143) cooked and served in broth, rather than in a heavier sauce.

Whole chicken eggs contain about 75 percent water. A large yolk measures a little less than 1 tablespoon (9 g) and contains about 2 teaspoons (10 ml) of water, all the fat and cholesterol, about 40 percent of the egg's protein, and most of its vitamins. The white measures a little more than 2 tablespoons (38 g) and contains about 2 tablespoons (30 ml) of water, with the rest almost entirely protein. The shell accounts for about 12 percent of the egg's total weight, but it is not included when measuring egg size.

SALMONELLA AND FRESH PASTA

There is very slight danger of salmonella contamination when making fresh pasta. Some authorities recommend refrigerating the noodles and using them within 2 days or freezing and using them within 2 months. In hot, humid weather, cover and refrigerate cut pasta strips and especially stuffed pasta to avoid any possibility of mold developing. If you are concerned or have a compromised immune system, consider using pasteurised shell eggs. But, in all cases, use the best-quality eggs you can find, avoiding cheap, mass-produced eggs, and keep them refrigerated until you're ready to start making pasta.

CHOOSING EGGS

Chicken breeds with white earlobes lay white eggs; chicken breeds with red earlobes lay brown eggs. Preferences are regional and cultural. If all else is equal, brown and white eggs taste the same and have the same nutritional content. Brown eggs come from larger breeds that eat more and take longer to produce an egg, so they develop thicker shells and are usually more expensive. I prefer brown eggs for pasta because I feel that their thicker shells help protect the egg and keep it fresher, plus they are just aesthetically more pleasing. In the United States, brown eggs are more of a specialty product, so quality tends to be higher. In the UK, brown eggs are preferred and more common. Any small brownish spots, which are prevalent in brown eggs, are harmless bits of protein.

Extra-fresh, extra-rich brown eggs labeled *speciali per pasta fatta in casa* (specially raised for making homemade pasta) are available in Italy. These have large, deep orange-red yolks that are higher in protein and lecithin, an emulsifier that lubricates and makes for smooth consistency. Eggs from pastured chickens that are free to roam will have the richest yolks and will usually be the freshest.

Egg yolks add structure, tenderness, and golden colour to pasta, and good, rich, fresh eggs are the secret of tender fresh sheet pasta. Egg yolks get their colour from carotenoids, which strengthen the hen's immune system. Because healthy hens only hatch their eggs if the yolks have sufficient carotenoids, deep-coloured yolks are a sign of a happy hen. A hen that eats a diet rich in carotenoid yellow-orange plant pigments such as marigold petals and yellow corn will produce eggs with deeper gold yolks than if she eats pale foods such as white cornmeal, barley, or, for at least one Italian producer, goat's milk.

ROSSO

In Italy, egg yolks are often deep orange and are known as the "red" (*rosso*) instead of the "yellow." Thirty yolks or more per kilo (14 yolks per pound) of flour may be used to make ultra-rich Piedmontese tajarin, and a similar amount is used to make tagliolini in Emilia.

Pastured and Araucana chicken eggs (left), duck eggs (right)

U.S. AND EUROPEAN EGG SIZES

U.S. Large	1.8 ounces, 50 grams each	**European Union Small**	1.9 ounces each, 53 grams and under
U.S. Extra-Large	2.25 ounces, 63 grams each	**European Union Medium**	1.9 to 2.2 ounces each, 53 to 63 grams
U.S. Jumbo	2.7 ounces, 75 grams each	**European Union Large**	2.2 to 2.6 ounces each, 63 to 73 grams

EGG GRADES AND SIZES

U.S. eggs are graded by shell thickness and firmness of the white. AA is the top grade, followed by A (most supermarket eggs), and B, with thin shells and watery whites. They are sized by the dozen and the weight is measured with the egg out of the shell. Large is the most common size in the United States. For European readers using these recipes, work with small or medium eggs if possible, and adjust the pasta dough recipes to account for larger size eggs by eliminating the water called for in the recipe.

In the UK and the European Union, eggs are graded A or B. Grade A eggs are clean, fresh, and internally perfect with an intact shell and an air pocket no larger than 6 mm (about ¼ inch) in depth. The yolk must not move away from the centre of the egg when it is rotated. Grade A eggs are sold in the shell and are individually stamped with a standardised code that indicates the type of farming system used and the country and place of origin, so any single egg can be traced through an unbroken chain to the farm where it was laid. Mostly for commercial and industrial uses, Grade B eggs are cracked, removed from their shells, and pasteurised before sale in containers.

FRESHNESS OF EGGS

As an egg ages, air forms a pocket in the empty space between the white and shell, usually (though not always) at the large end. A fresh egg will have little to no air pocket. The yolk will be rich in colour and will stand upright, and the white will be thick and firm and hold its shape. Fresh egg whites are cloudy because they contain carbon dioxide. As the egg white ages, it thins out and becomes more transparent. Eggs with blood spots, caused by the rupture of blood vessels, are perfectly safe and do not indicate that the egg has been fertilised. (These days, hens are kept far from roosters, and eggs are rarely fertilised.)

In the European Union eggs may only be sold within 21 days of hatching, and the "best before" date for fresh hen eggs is 28 days after laying. However, freshly laid eggs don't develop their appealing flavour until 3 days after laying. Up to day 9, eggs can be marketed with a sleeve marked "Extra" or "Extra Fresh." From day 10 on, they must be stored in a cool, dark, and dry place. After day 18, eggs must be kept refrigerated.

ITLALIAN GOAT'S MILK–FED CHICKEN

Heritage Gallina Livornese breed chickens from producer Paolo Parisi of Pisa eat grains and goat's milk. The resulting eggs have a delicate almond flavour, soft, rich, light yolks, and strong protein structure. They are particularly appreciated for making light fresh pasta. The Caponi Company, a small-scale pasta producer also in Pisa, uses Parisi's eggs to produce specially marked packages of tagliatelle made from semolina and 23 percent egg.

WHEAT

Wheat, various species within the genus *Triticum*, is an annual grass, which has been cultivated since prehistoric times. The simplest wheat is einkorn, which has two sets of chromosomes. About a million years ago, wild wheat mated with wild goatgrass and developed four sets of chromosomes and two of the Mediterranean region's important types of wheat: emmer (or farro) and durum.

About 8,000 years ago, a further mating between tetraploid wheat and goatgrass gave us modern bread wheat, *Triticum aestivum*, with six sets of chromosomes. The extra chromosomes are thought to contribute to the diversity of modern wheats. Ninety percent of the wheat grown in the world today is hexaploid (six chromosome) bread wheat. Most of the remaining 10 percent is durum wheat, *Triticum durum*, used mainly for making dried pasta. Others types of wheat, such as spelt and emmer, are cultivated on a much smaller scale.

Wheat kernels are commonly reddish brown in colour because chemical compounds called "phenols" in the outer bran layer are transformed into pigments by enzymes. White wheat, a naturally occurring albino variety, is lower in phenols and milder in flavour. Durum wheat is golden yellow because it contains the antioxidant carotenoid pigment, lutein, which is also present in egg yolks.

For homemade pasta, lower-protein, extra-finely milled flour is preferred in Italian homes because it is easiest to roll out and results in soft, tender pasta that readily absorbs sauce or broth. For restaurants and fresh pasta shops, the dough often includes durum flour or semolina to make the pasta more durable and less likely to stick. Chinese noodle makers also prefer soft wheat, and until recently, China didn't grow durum wheat. High-protein durum wheat is used for industrial dried pasta, usually made with water and no eggs, and doughs for some specialty handmade pasta such as orecchiette. Because

PARTS OF THE WHEAT KERNEL

The wheat kernel has three main parts: the husk, the endosperm, and the germ.

Husk	Represents about 14 percent of the kernel's weight; removed for white flour and included in whole wheat flour. Sold separately as bran and contains a small amount of protein, large quantities of B vitamins, trace minerals, and dietary fibre, mostly insoluble.
Endosperm	Represents about 83 percent of the kernel's weight and is the source of white flour. Contains most of the wheat's protein, carbohydrates and iron, B-vitamins, and soluble fibre. About 80 percent of its protein is gluten. When gluten mixes with water, proteins bond together, forming an elastic mass that can expand to hold the gas bubbles produced by yeast or make it stretchable to see-through thickness for pasta dough.
Germ	Also known as the embryo, this sprouting part is the smallest part of the wheat kernel, representing only about 2.5 percent of its weight. Often removed from flour in milling because the fat it contains (10 percent) leads to rancidity if not kept refrigerated. Wheat germ, which is included in whole wheat flour, contains small quantities of high-quality protein, B vitamins, and trace minerals.

PROTEIN PERCENTAGES OF FLOUR

To determine the protein percentage of flour, divide the protein content listed on the label (usually 3 to 5 grams) by the number of grams per serving (usually 30 to 35). Flour with a protein content of 4 grams per 30-gram serving is 13 percent protein. This makes it easier to compare protein contents among different brands and types of flour. Flour that is higher in protein will absorb more liquid.

the protein content of wheat varies from year to year, commercial flours are blended for consistency.

If you have access to freshly milled locally grown wheat, try making your dough with that for its wheaty flavour and fragrance, and often enhanced nutrients, adjusting the liquid quantities as needed.

Hard red wheat is used to produce flour high in gluten, or bread flour. Soft red wheat yields flour that is low in gluten and known as pastry flour, the type used for pasta. Unfortunately, most mainstream supermarkets don't sell pastry flour, just bread and all-purpose flour. I have used Italian 00 or all-purpose (U.S. standard) for many recipes in this book. If you are able to get pastry flour, it is an excellent substitute and will result in tender texture. You will generally need to decrease the amount of liquid if using pastry flour, as with its lower protein content (usually 8 to 10 percent), it will absorb less liquid.

MEASURING FLOUR

In much of the world, recipes are done by weight, which is much more accurate than U.S. recipes with their volume measures. While liquids are standard in volume and weight, solids, especially porous flour, range in volume according to humidity, aging, and measuring method. Every brand and milling method yields flour with a different consistency and 1 cup may range in weight from 120 to 160 grams (4.2 to 5.6 ounces).

I have developed the recipes in this book using weight in both U.S. and metric measurements. I recommend using a digital scale to weigh your flour for results that you'll be able to easily duplicate time and again. To best measure flour without a scale, stir or whisk the flour to break up any lumps, spoon into a cup without packing down, then level the cup with a knife or other straight edge. Compensate by adding more flour or more egg as needed to obtain dough with the perfect firm but yielding consistency, and refer to the conversion chart (page 170) if you don't have a scale.

MORE ABOUT GLUTEN

Gluten is a composite of two insoluble proteins, glutenin and gliadin. Glutenin, one of the largest of proteins, provides structure and elasticity, developing a stable three-dimensional network connecting protein molecules during the kneading process. Gliadin, a plant storage protein, is viscous and extensible, allowing the dough to be rolled out and providing bite and firmness to the dough.

ASH CONTENT AND EXTRACTION RATE IN FLOUR

The outer layers of the wheat kernel contain the highest concentration of minerals, which darken the colour of the flour and impart a stronger flavour; the inner layers are lowest in minerals and are lighter in colour and milder in flavour. Flour that is high in minerals ferments more easily, ideal for bread but ill-suited to pasta. Especially in Europe, flour may be labeled with its ash content, determined by incinerating a 100-gram (3.5-ounce) sample and measuring the ash. Whole wheat flour leaves about 2 grams (0.07 ounce) of ash; white flour about 0.4 grams (0.01 ounce). Flour is also categorised by its extraction rate: whole wheat flour has a 100 percent extraction rate - everything that comes out of the grinder goes into the flour; American white flour is typically milled at a 72 percent extraction rate.

TYPES OF WHEAT FLOUR

Italian Doppio Zero (00)

In Italy, flour is milled to various degrees of fineness from 2, the coarsest, to 000, the finest. The number of zeros is unrelated to gluten content. There is 00 flour meant for bread (labeled *panifiabile* in Italian), for pizza, and for pasta with gluten levels ranging from 5 to 12 percent. In the North, 00 flour produced from soft wheat (*grano tenero*) and relatively low in protein is preferred for making fresh pasta at home. Some pasta artisans choose slightly grainier 0 flour, and others add some durum flour or semolina for colour and strength, as I do in my mix.

Look for imported extra-fine Italian doppio zero flour from specialty Italian importers. Molino Caputo, a mill in Naples that specialises in slow-ground artisan flours, produces a special 00 flour labeled "Pasta Fresca and Gnocchi" that is ideal for fresh pasta but not easy to find in the United States.

Unbleached All-Purpose

This is wheat flour with a moderate gluten level, usually 9 to 12 percent protein. It is often a blend of high-protein bread flour and lower-protein pastry flour, but it may be milled from a single moderate-protein wheat variety. (Some regional all-purpose flours are lower in protein at 7.5 to 9.5 percent.) "AP flour" works well for pasta either on its own or combined with other flours and ingredients. Unbleached flour is aged naturally by allowing the flour to oxidise slowly with oxygen in the air. I avoid using chemically treated bleached flour. In hot weather, store unbleached flour in the refrigerator or freezer, but bring it to room temperature before making pasta.

Durum and Semolina

Durum, or macaroni wheat, *Triticum durum*, developed in the Middle East and spread to the Mediterranean before Roman times. It grows best in semiarid climates, whether hot as in Southern Italy or cold as in Canada. Today, the great majority grown is amber durum with large translucent amber-coloured grains. High protein content and strong extensible, but not elastic, gluten makes durum especially good to form the intricate shapes of extruded dry pasta.

Semolina, the glassy inner endosperm of durum wheat, is hard, grainy, and golden yellow in colour with mellow nutty flavour. Semolina itself is milled in various grades of fineness; the finer, the better for pasta. Pale yellow grainy durum flour is a finer-textured by-product of semolina production and is slightly higher in protein.

Fresh pasta may be made from all or part durum flour for chewy texture, stretchability, and nutty flavour, though the dough will absorb more liquid and will be firmer and more difficult to roll out than if made with soft wheat. Durum flour is not usually available in supermarkets. Look for it in Italian and other specialty stores or order it (see Resources, page 168).

Durum is more expensive than other wheats, and formerly in Italy, only the most expensive dried pasta was made from it. Today, by Italian law, commercial pasta must be made from 100 percent durum semolina.

PASTA FLOUR MIX

For many of the pasta doughs in this book, I use a blend of unbleached all-purpose flour, durum flour, and semolina. Some flour companies produce their own proprietary pasta flour blends using durum and semolina or a blend of three flours. One American company, Ecco La Pasta, even makes pasta flour that includes dried egg so all you add is water, though I prefer to add fresh eggs myself.

½ pound (225 g) unbleached all-purpose flour
¼ pound (115 g) durum flour
¼ pound (115 g) semolina

Yield: 1 pound (450 g)

BULK RECIPE FOR PASTA FLOUR MIX

4 pounds (2 kg) unbleached all-purpose flour
2 pounds (900 g) durum flour
2 pounds (900 g) semolina

Yield: 8 pounds (3.6 kg)

Combine in a bowl and whisk together to mix evenly. Store covered and dry, refrigerated in hot weather.

Whole Wheat

Whole wheat flour is made by stone-grinding or steel-rolling the entire grain or kernel of wheat: bran, endosperm, and germ. With its brownish, speckled look, whole wheat flour has full-bodied flavour, texture, and fibre as well as naturally occurring vitamins and minerals. Because the outer bran contains tannin, whole wheat has a bold, slightly bitter taste. Mild white whole wheat flour is ivory to cream in colour. (In the UK, whole wheat flour is generally made from white whole wheat.) All whole wheat flours tend to get rancid and/or buggy easily because of the rich oils contained in wheat germ. Store in the refrigerator or freezer, especially in hot weather, and check any packaged flour for a rancid smell before using. Bring flour to room temperature before making pasta.

Spelt

Spelt, *Triticum aestivum spelta*, is an important wheat subspecies in southern Germany, where it is known as *dinkel* and where it has been grown since 4000 BCE. Spelt kernels are notoriously hard and require special equipment for milling. The tough husk is removed before milling. Spelt is high in fibre and protein with a sweet flavour. The gluten in spelt may be better tolerated than common wheat by people with gluten sensitivities. Although spelt flour is high in protein, the gluten it contains is quite fragile, so pasta made from spelt will tend to be crumbly and is best rolled out thicker than normal.

Farro

Farro, or emmer wheat, *Triticum turgidum dicoccum*, was the most important cultivated wheat in the Middle East and the Mediterranean region until Roman times, when durum and bread wheats took over. Flour made from farro is used to make artisan pasta, especially in Tuscany and Umbria. Though farro is high in protein, a large portion is nongluten-forming so the pasta made from it will tend to be crumbly.

Farro grain and flour

Italian chestnut flour, chestnuts, and sage leaves

OTHER FLOURS

Chestnut

Chestnut flour goes into specialty pasta and dumplings such as Genoese Chestnut Corzetti (page 120), gnocchi, and spaetzle. To produce the light-tan clumpy flour, kernels of European chestnuts, *Castanea sativa*, are peeled, dried, and ground. The resulting flour is sweet and dense with notes of hazelnut and vanilla. In Tuscany, chestnuts are roasted over a chestnut wood fire before grinding, developing an intense smoky sweetness and darker cappuccino colour. In the United States, small amounts of chestnut flour from hybrid American-Asian chestnuts are now being produced but sell out quickly. Chestnut flour contains no gluten, so it is mixed about 1 to 3 with white flour. Handle chestnut flour pasta gently because its low gluten content makes for fragile pasta. Store chestnut flour refrigerated or frozen. Bring to room temperature before use.

Lighter Italian and darker U.S. buckwheat flours

Buckwheat

Buckwheat, *Fagopyrum esculentum*, a member of the rhubarb and sorrel family unrelated to wheat, is native to Siberia and thrives in cold climates and poor soil. A staple of the mountainous regions of Northern Japan, buckwheat is an important crop in Alpine Italy and France. Italian buckwheat flour is usually lighter in colour and more coarsely ground than American. Buckwheat contains no gluten, so it's mixed with wheat flour for pasta dough, but it may be a dangerous allergen on its own.

Rye

Rye, *Secale cereale*, has been cultivated in Central and Eastern Europe and Western Russia since about the fifth century and may have traveled west from Turkey along with wheat. Dough made with rye will be sticky because the special carbohydrates contained in rye absorb large amounts of water: about eight times its weight versus two times for wheat. Store rye in the freezer but bring to room temperature before use.

Chickpea

Chickpea flour (*farina di ceci* in Italian) is delicately ground from dried and roasted or unroasted chickpeas. The unroasted type is used for pasta and dumplings. Look for chickpea flour under its Indian names, gram or besan flour, or its Spanish name, garbanzo flour. Because it contains no gluten, chickpea flour is mixed 1 to 3 with wheat flour for pasta.

Rice

Rice flour is finely milled rice and may be made from either whole grain brown rice or hulled white rice. Rice flour consists mostly of starch with a small amount of protein. In Asia, especially Japan and southern China, light, almost transparent noodles and dumplings such as wonton are made from rice flour rather than wheat flour, or a combination of flours. It is often substituted for wheat flour for those who are gluten-intolerant.

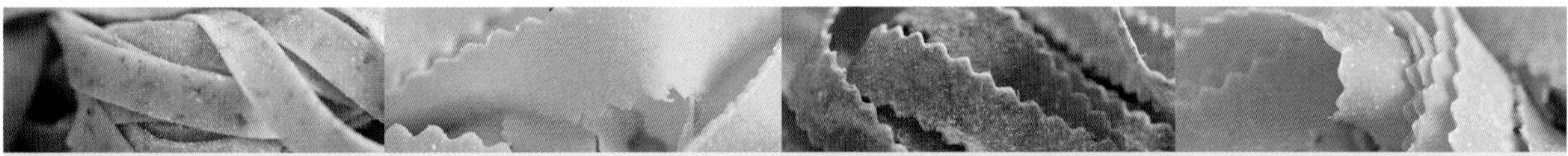

GRINDING WHOLE GRAINS FOR FLOUR

YOU CAN GRIND your own whole wheat flour or other grain for freshness or perhaps when a specialty flour is not available. It is simple with a grain grinder or a grain grinder attachment for a standing mixer.

To grind flour, use the finest setting on the grinder, and do not grind more than ½ pound (225 g) at a time. (The motor can overheat if you try to grind more.) Here, we grind barley flour, but you can grind whole wheat berries, chickpeas, or other grains and legumes the same way.

Pour ½ pound (225 g) of pearled barley kernels, which have been polished to remove the hulls, onto a shallow tray. Inspect for any small stones or hardened bits of dirt and remove.

Add the barley to the grain mill hopper and place a large bowl underneath the chute to catch the flour. Grind the barley, which will happen rather slowly.

You may wish to strain the resulting flour to remove larger bits of skin. Transfer to a fine wire sieve that has been placed over another large bowl. Shake to encourage the ground bits to pass through the sieve, rubbing the surface in a clockwise motion with your hand (counterclockwise if you're left-handed) until only large flecks are left. Discard the pieces and the flour is ready to use. Store tightly sealed and refrigerated or frozen, but bring it to room temperature before making pasta.

Make barley flour by grinding whole pearled barley on the finest setting of a grain grinder.

CHAPTER TWO

MAKING PASTA DOUGH FROM WHEAT AND OTHER FLOURS

WE CAN MAKE pasta dough by hand on a wooden board or in a bowl; we can make it by machine using a standing mixer with a strong motor or a food processor. The basic flour and egg dough may be varied by using Italian 00 flour for the most tender dough, unbleached all-purpose flour for a slightly firmer dough, a pasta flour blend with the chewiness of durum and semolina, or semolina flour for rustic dough with firm bite. The eggs may be whole, all yolks, or a combination of whole eggs, whites, or yolks with another liquid such as water or white wine. In this chapter, you'll learn all about making that dough, usually in batches of about 1 pound (450 g), enough to serve 4 to 6 people, and yielding about 2 pounds (900 g) when cooked, depending on how dry it is and the size and shape of the cut.

MASTERING THE ART OF MAKING PASTA DOUGH

■ The higher the protein content of the flour, the more water (or egg) it will absorb. The lower the humidity, the more liquid will be needed for the dough and the quicker the dough will dry out. In dry weather, increase the ambient humidity in your kitchen so the pasta doesn't crack. Use a humidifier or fill a large pot with water and keep it boiling, refilling as needed.

■ To check if the dough has the proper proportion of flour to liquid, press your thumb into the centre of the ball of dough - it should come out clean. If the dough is too wet, work in more flour. To add more liquid or flour to an already prepared dough, cut the dough into ½-inch (1-cm) cubes and toss with liquid or flour and knead until smooth. Or, to add small amounts of liquid, spray the surface with water from a mister and knead until the liquid has been absorbed. Allow the dough to rest at least 30 minutes after adding water or liquid to relax the gluten and make the dough easier to roll.

■ If you are using a mechanical sheeter, it is not necessary to fully knead the dough because the action of running the dough through the sheeter also kneads it. Instead, knead until it is cohesive and moderately smooth, about 5 minutes. If rolling by hand, the

Facing page: **Hand-stretched pasta dough**

dough must be fully kneaded until smooth and elastic, about 10 minutes. To check if the dough has been kneaded long enough for hand-rolling, cut it open: You should see small air bubbles inside and on the surface.

■ Use ingredients at room temperature when making pasta so the flour is absorbed more readily and the dough is easier to knead. Warm eggs by placing them in a bowl of slightly hot water (110°F, or 43°C) for 5 to 8 minutes. Warm flour if it has been chilled or frozen by placing it in a bowl and microwaving briefly (15 seconds at a time) until it reaches room temperature.

■ When working with pasta dough, as with yeast-raised dough, it's best to knead and roll out on wood, which tends to be warm, not marble or granite, which tend to be cold.

■ Do not undervalue patience - allow the kneaded pasta dough to rest at least 30 minutes before rolling. This hydrates it so the flour is completely absorbed and the dough becomes softer and easier to roll. (If using grainy semolina, allow the dough to rest at least 1 hour.) The gluten that you have developed in the kneading process will relax and the dough won't spring back.

■ Even though pasta dough will continue to soften as it rests and absorbs flour, once stretched out, the pasta will not get soft and mushy when cooked. The strength of the protein bonds that form as the pasta cooks compensates for any loss of elasticity from dough that has softened.

■ In hot, humid weather, place a table fan on low speed near the pasta drying on racks or trays for air circulation. Turn the pasta sheets several times so they dry out evenly without developing any mold before forming into nests and drying fully. Turn stuffed pasta such as ravioli after 30 minutes to prevent sticking. Or, once the pasta has been cut and formed into portion-size nests, arrange on a tray that has been covered with waxed paper or parchment paper and sprinkled with semolina or cornmeal, cover with plastic wrap, and store refrigerated up to 3 days.

BASIC EGG PASTA DOUGH BY HAND

Here we make Basic Egg Pasta Dough by hand to use either in the sheeter or for hand-rolling. In Italy, pasta dough is made in quantities determined by the egg count. My standard restaurant recipe starts with 36 eggs. Here we make two-egg and three-egg batches, perfect for the home cook.

TWO-EGG BASIC PASTA DOUGH
(Best Quantity for Hand-Rolling)

If you'll be hand-rolling the dough, add 1 to 2 tablespoons (15 to 30 ml) more water to make a softer, pliable, silky dough that's easy to roll and stretch.

½ pound (225 g) Pasta Flour Mix (page 24), unbleached all-purpose flour, 00 flour, or Korean flour
2 large eggs, at room temperature
1 egg yolk
1 to 2 tablespoons (15 to 30 ml) tepid water
Extra flour plus semolina for rolling

Yield: about ¾ pound (350 g), serves 3 to 4

THREE-EGG BASIC PASTA DOUGH
(Best Quantity for Machine-Rolling)

If you wish to hand-roll this dough, divide it into 2 sections and roll each separately.

¾ pound (350 g) Pasta Flour Mix (page 24), unbleached all-purpose flour, 00 flour, or Korean flour
3 large eggs, at room temperature
1 egg yolk
2 to 3 tablespoons (30 to 45 ml) tepid water

Yield: about 18 ounces (500 g), serves 5 to 6

ALL-YOLK PASTA DOUGH
(Best for Hand-Rolling)

This extra-rich golden dough is suitable for Tortellini (page 143) or for Tagliolini (page 106).

½ pound (225 g) Pasta Flour Mix (page 24), unbleached all-purpose flour, 00 flour, or Korean flour
8 egg yolks, at room temperature
3 to 4 tablespoons (45 to 60 ml) tepid water

Yield: about ¾ pound (350 g), serves 3 to 4

1 Mound the flour in the centre of a large wooden board or other work surface or in a large bowl to form a flour "volcano" with a "crater" in the middle. Pour the eggs and water into the crater **(A)**. (For the all-yolk dough, lightly beat together the yolks and water in a small bowl, then pour into the crater.)

2 Using a table fork, begin to incorporate the flour, starting with the inner rim **(B)**.

As more flour gets incorporated, push the flour up to maintain the crater shape so the egg doesn't run out. (If the egg does run out, scrape up the liquid with a bench scraper or the side of a spatula and add it back into the mass.)

3 If using the bowl, once about half the flour has been incorporated and the mixture has formed a shaggy mass, transfer the dough to a work surface, preferably a wooden board **(C)**.

4 Dust the board lightly with flour and begin to knead the dough **(D)**. Keep incorporating the flour, turning the dough mass over several times while kneading so that the moist side of the dough is exposed to the flour, encouraging the flour to be absorbed. Scrape up and discard any leftover hard bits of dough.

A
B
C
D

5 Use the heel of your palm to push the dough down and away, then fold the edge back over top to keep a basically round dough ball **(E)**. Rotate the dough mass clockwise about 90 degrees each time if you are left-handed and counterclockwise if right-handed.

6 Continue kneading the dough about 5 minutes, or until the dough is cohesive and moderately smooth. (Running the dough through the pasta sheeter will develop the gluten further, making it smooth and elastic.) If making stuffed pasta, the dough should stick lightly to your fingers. For pasta to be cut in sheets or in strips, add enough extra flour to make a firmer dough that releases easily from your fingers.

7 The small bubbles that start to appear on the surface are a sign that the gluten has developed completely and the dough has been sufficiently kneaded **(F)**.

E

8 Form the dough into a smooth, round ball, pulling from the outside to the centre on the bottom, so the bottom portion joins together in the centre and the top is completely smooth **(G & H)**.

Cover the dough with a bowl or a damp cloth, or wrap it in plastic and allow it to rest for 30 minutes at room temperature before rolling. The dough will continue to absorb flour as it rests and relaxes.

NOTES: If you're right-handed, beat the egg counterclockwise while using your left hand to support the volcano, keeping the egg from running out. If you're left-handed, beat the egg clockwise while using your right hand to support the volcano. Overflowing egg can make a big mess if made using the table but is not much of a problem if made using the bowl.

For hand-rolled pasta, knead until the dough is completely smooth and elastic, about 10 minutes. (The dough for hand-rolling should be soft and supple, softer than for machine-rolling.)

F

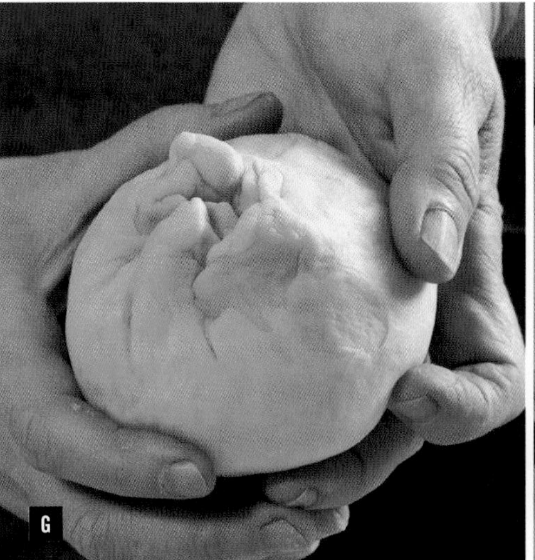
G

H

BASIC EGG PASTA DOUGH USING A HEAVY-DUTY STAND MIXER

Because pasta dough is quite dense, this is the largest batch that will work effectively without overheating or even burning out the mixer's motor unless you have a commercial machine with a stronger motor. As soon as the dough ball forms, remove it from the bowl and continue kneading by hand on a wooden work surface. If you really want to knead in the machine, divide the dough in half and knead in 2 batches, then combine by kneading briefly by hand.

¾ pound (350 g) Pasta Flour Mix (page 24), unbleached all-purpose flour, Italian 00 flour, or Korean flour
3 large eggs, at room temperature
1 egg yolk
2 to 3 tablespoons (30 to 45 ml) tepid water

Yield: about 18 ounces (500 g), serves 5 to6

1. Place the flour in the bowl of a standing mixer (other mixers don't have a motor that is powerful enough to make pasta dough) fitted with the paddle attachment. Add the eggs while beating on low speed and beat until the mixture forms moist crumbs **(A)**.

2. Add the water 1 tablespoon (15 ml) at a time, adding enough for the dough to come together and form large moist crumbs. If the crumbs are dry with flour on their surface, add a little more water **(B)**.

3. Keep beating until the dough comes together to form a mass that comes away cleanly from the side of the bowl **(C)**.

A

B

C

4 To ensure that the stiff dough doesn't damage the motor and the bowl doesn't jump out of its holder, grasp the side of the bowl while beating and turn off the motor immediately if you hear any grinding of the gears **(D)**.

5 Remove the dough from the mixer and transfer to a wooden work surface **(E)**. (Some loose flour may remain at the bottom of the mixer bowl.)

6 Mix the dough well with your hands to incorporate any loose flour **(F)**.

7 Knead on a wooden work surface by pushing away with the palms of your hands **(G)**.

8 Fold the front edge of the dough over, then knead again. Rotate the dough 90 degrees and then repeat, kneading the dough until it is cohesive and moderately smooth, about 5 minutes **(H)**.

Cover the dough with a bowl or a damp cloth, or cover in plastic wrap and allow it to rest for at least 30 minutes at room temperature to relax the gluten and allow the flour to be fully absorbed by the liquid.

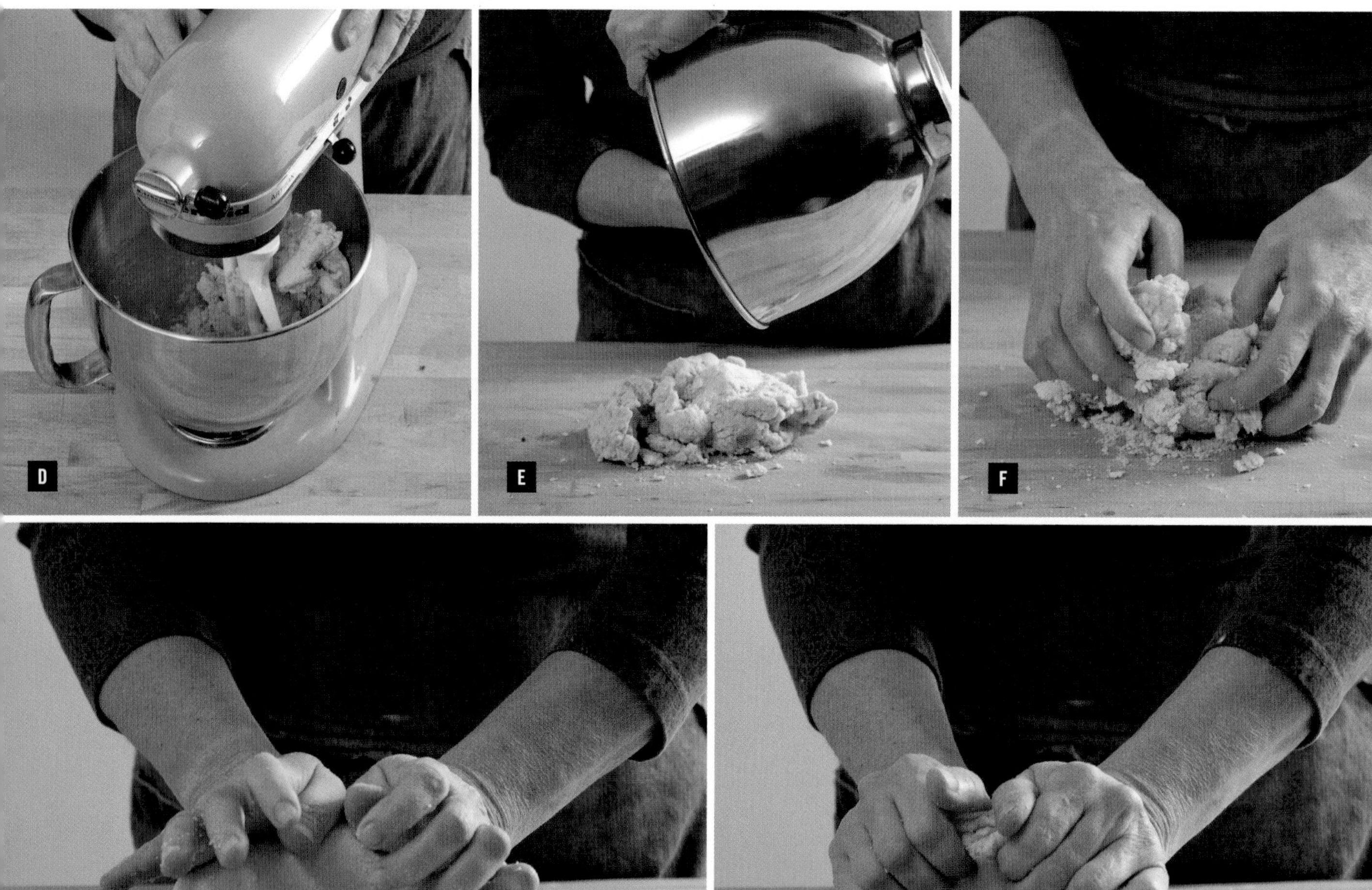
D E F G H

BASIC EGG PASTA DOUGH USING A FOOD PROCESSOR

When using a food processor to make dough, the easiest way is to start with the dry ingredients (the flour) and start adding the liquid (eggs and water) until the dough absorbs enough liquid to form a mass. Stay by the machine while it is processing as you do not want to burn out the motor by letting the fully formed dough mass continue to beat.

¾ pound (350 g) Pasta Flour Mix (page 24), unbleached all-purpose flour, Italian 00 flour, or Korean flour
3 large eggs, at room temperature
1 egg yolk
2 to 3 tablespoons (30 to 45 ml) tepid water

Yield: about 1¼ pounds (565 g), serves 6 to 8

1. Place the flour in the bowl of a food processor. In a small bowl or measuring cup, lightly beat together the eggs and water.
2. Start adding the liquid to the flour through the pouring spout with the machine running. The dough will start to form small moist clumps **(A)**.
3. Continue adding liquid and processing until the mixture comes together to form a rough mass **(B)**. Stop the machine at this point because you might burn out the motor if you continue.
4. Remove the dough from the processor and transfer to a work surface, preferably wood **(C)**.

A

B

C

5 Dust the board lightly with flour and knead the dough until it is cohesive and moderately smooth, about 5 minutes **(D)**. Running the dough through the pasta sheeter will develop the gluten further, making it smooth and elastic.

6 Cover the dough with a bowl, a damp towel, or plastic wrap and allow it to rest at room temperature for 30 minutes to relax the dough before proceeding with rolling **(E)**.

D

E

Dough that has discoloured on the outside has oxidised and/or fermented so that it contains large bubbles. It should be discarded.

USING OTHER FLOURS TO **MAKE PASTA DOUGHS**

While pasta dough made from 100 percent wheat flour will be highest in gluten and therefore less likely to be brittle, other flours add interesting texture, colour, flavour, and increased nutritional value. In this section, I combine wheat flour with other flours including whole wheat, buckwheat, rye, cornmeal, and semolina.

WHOLE WHEAT PASTA DOUGH

Whole wheat contains rough particles that interfere with the gluten strands, so mix equal parts of whole wheat with white flour. The pasta will be brittle when dry, so handle with care. Whole wheat pasta dough pairs best with light but earthy sauces such as the traditional Venetian onion and anchovy sauce and mushroom, meat, or duck ragù. Fresh beans such as cranberry and/or sharp, peppery greens like broccoli rabe, arugula, or turnip greens are good choices. Cream obscures the pasta's warm brown colour so dress with butter or olive oil instead.

6 ounces (170 g) whole wheat flour, the finer the grind the better
6 ounces (170 g) Pasta Flour Mix (page 24)
2 large eggs, at room temperature
1 egg white
6 tablespoons (90 ml) tepid water

Yield: about 18 ounces (500 g), serves 5 to 6

Combine both flours and form the "volcano." Lightly beat together the eggs and water and pour into the "crater" in the centre. Knead 5 minutes by hand following the directions in Basic Egg Pasta Dough on page 32 until the dough is cohesive and moderately smooth.

NOTE: Because of the whole wheat flour it contains, this dough will suck up moisture. Add more water, 1 tablespoon (15 ml) at a time, until the dough comes together to form a firm but not hard ball that doesn't stick to your fingers.

Buckwheat pasta pizzoccheri

BUCKWHEAT PASTA DOUGH

Buckwheat contains no gluten, so mix this dark, earthy flour with durum flour for strength. Even so, it will be fragile, so don't try to roll it out too thin.

¼ pound (115 g) buckwheat flour
½ pound (225 g) durum wheat flour, plus extra for rolling
4 large eggs, at room temperature
1 to 2 tablespoons (15 to 30 ml) tepid water

Yield: 1¼ pounds (565 g), serves 6 to 8

Combine flours and form the "volcano." Lightly beat together the eggs and water and pour into the "crater" in the centre. Using a fork, gradually mix in the flour until the mixture forms a cohesive mass. Continue mixing in the flour while kneading. Knead 5 minutes by hand following the directions in Basic Egg Pasta Dough on page 32 until the dough is cohesive and moderately smooth.

Rye pasta reginette

RYE PASTA DOUGH

Rye is softer and stickier than wheat and should be rolled out thicker than wheat dough. Mix rye with durum flour to add strength and to mellow its flavour. Caraway is a typical flavouring for rye bread and also works well for pasta.

¼ pound (115 g) or 4 ounces dark rye flour
½ pound (225 g) or 8 ounces durum flour, plus extra for rolling
1 teaspoon finely ground caraway seed (use a spice grinder), optional
3 large eggs, at room temperature
3 to 4 tablespoons (45 to 60 ml) tepid water

Yield: about 18 ounces (500 g), serves 5 to 6

Mound the rye flour, durum, and ground caraway in the centre of a large wooden cutting board or in a large bowl to form a "volcano" with a "crater" in the middle. Pour the eggs into the crater, and, using a fork, begin to incorporate the flour, starting with the inner rim. Follow the directions in Basic Egg Pasta Dough on page 31 to complete the dough.

Cornmeal-chipotle pasta triangles

CORNMEAL-CHIPOTLE PASTA DOUGH

This is a decidedly nontraditional pasta dough with the Latino accent of smoked chipotle chiles mixed with cornmeal. In Italy, corn was long considered a lowly food of the poor and the Jews and was mostly eaten in the form of polenta rather than pasta. Substitute 1 to 2 teaspoons of ground chipotle for the chipotle in adobo (found in small cans with Mexican food).

¼ pound (115 g) stone-ground yellow cornmeal
½ pound (225 g) durum flour
4 large eggs, at room temperature
1 tablespoon (15 g) seeded and finely chopped chipotle in adobo, including sauce

Yield: about 1 pound (450 g), serves 4 to 6

Mound the cornmeal and flour in the centre of a large wooden cutting board or in a large bowl to form a flour "volcano" with a "crater" in the middle. Pour the eggs and chopped chipotles into the crater, and, using a fork, begin to incorporate the flour, starting with the inner rim. Complete the dough following the directions in Basic Egg Pasta Dough on page 31.

SEMOLINA PASTA DOUGH

This is a firm, nutty dough with a pleasing yellow colour that works well for rustic-style pasta such as Abruzzese Pasta alla Chitarra (page 108) or Roman tonnarelli, square-cut long pasta. Because durum semolina is high in protein, the dough is best rolled by machine. Allow this dough to rest about 1 hour before rolling, so the flour completely absorbs the liquid, becoming softer and smoother.

¼ pound (115 g) semolina
½ pound (225 g) durum flour
3 large eggs, at room temperature
1 to 2 tablespoons (15 to 30 ml) tepid water

Yield: about 1 pound (450 g), serves 4 to 6

Mound the semolina and durum flour in the centre of a large wooden cutting board or in a large bowl to form a flour "volcano" with a "crater" in the middle. Pour the eggs and water into the crater, and, using a fork, begin to incorporate the flour, starting with the inner rim. Complete the dough following the directions in Basic Egg Pasta Dough on page 31.

METHODS FOR **FORMING PASTA**

Rolling the dough out by hand on wood using a wooden rolling pin makes a superb product with a textured rather than completely smooth surface that can't be produced any other way. However, this method requires patience, practice, and strength.

Using a hand-cranked pasta sheeter to thin the dough is an easier way of rolling out pasta dough.

You may cut the sheets of rolled-out pasta by hand or using any of the cutter attachments. The cutters range in width from the finest capelli d'angelo (angel hair) to square-cut trenette and fettuccine or tagliatelle (medium strips) to pappardelle and lasagne (wide strips). Some cutters have ridged edges, some straight edges. There's even a special cutter for making rounded spaghettini (thin spaghetti). If you end up making lots of pasta, you may wish to invest in an electric motor attachment for the machine.

The earliest mechanical home model pasta sheeter was made by the Vitantonio Manufacturing Company in 1906, the same year Fante's, the kitchenware shop still located in Philadelphia's historic Italian Market, was founded. If you visit, make sure to view their collection of antique pasta machines and tools above the pasta section.

HANDMADE PASTA TIPS

- Cut a straight edge from the front end of the rolled-out sheet to make it easier to thread into the machine.

- When making pasta dough for rolling in a sheeter, firmer is better. You will need to add less flour while working the dough and it will stick less, especially once the opening between the rollers is thinner. The firmer the dough, the higher the number you can roll to and the thinner the resulting pasta.

- When drying pasta, do not let the cut pasta strips touch, or they will stick together.

- Dry pasta sheets until they are dry on the surface with the texture of smooth cardboard but not brittle. The sheets are dried enough if the cut edges are whitish in colour.

- Most pasta doughs freeze well, especially those containing vegetable purées, because the acid in the vegetables helps maintain colour and fresh flavour. Egg dough tends to discolour in the freezer; all-yolk dough holds its colour better.

  To freeze, place the dough ball in a plastic resealable freezer bag and remove the air. For best quality, vacuum-seal before freezing. Defrost several hours or overnight in the refrigerator. In a pinch, remove dough from the bag, transfer to a microwavable bowl, and microwave at 10 percent power a minute at a time unless mostly defrosted. If the dough is in good condition with bright colour, you may refreeze it. If the dough is wet on the outside - water tends to migrate to the surface - pat it dry before rolling out.

This cast-iron pasta maker, stamped Gangemi and Renna Company of Philadelphia, is located at a small museum of kitchen tools at Tenuta Vannulo in Campania, Italy.

ROLLING PASTA WITH WOOD

- Pasta dough loves wood - roll the dough out on wood using a wooden rolling pin.
- Have ready a wooden work surface large enough to roll out a circle of dough about 3 feet (1 m) in diameter.
- Have ready a long straight pasta rolling pin about 2 inches (5 cm) in diameter and 2 to 3 feet (60 cm to 1 m) in length - the longer the pin, the larger the sheet you can roll but the more difficult it will be to handle.
- Italian rolling pins are generally made from heavy oak in Emilia-Romagna and from lighter beech wood in Umbria and Tuscany. I find the beech wood type easier to use. (See Resources on page 168 for retailers.) A thick, smooth wooden dowel or a French-style straight rolling pin makes the best substitute.

HAND-STRETCHED **PASTA DOUGH**

To make dough for rolling by hand, the dough should be softer and richer than if using the sheeter. For tagliolini or tortellini, you may wish to use all egg yolks. The finer the pasta will be cut, the richer the dough should be.

The dough for hand-rolling should be supple and tacky to the touch. If you use low-protein flour such as pastry flour, 00 flour, or Korean flour, you'll need to add less water, and the dough will be easier to roll out, though it may tend to tear if rolled out very thin or used for stuffed pasta. U.S. all-purpose flour will absorb more water and will take more effort to roll out because it is higher in gluten protein. AP flour often contains bread flour, which has more of the type of gluten that is stretchable but tends to snap back, rather than the extensible gluten in the 00 flour. (See Endosperm on page 22 for more.)

The dough for hand-stretched pasta must be kneaded until smooth and elastic with tiny blisters on the surface. By fully developing its stretchable gluten, you'll be able to roll out the dough into a thin sheet. Don't worry if your hand-stretched dough tears a bit or isn't completely smooth and even in thickness. This skill and ease will come with practice.
It's easier to knead and roll out a smaller amount of dough, especially for a beginner, so the recipes below make small batches. The length of the rolling pin

A

B

determines the size of the dough sheet you can roll out. The larger the pin, the bigger the sheet.

Here you can use Two-Egg Basic Pasta Dough (page 30) or All-Yolk Pasta Dough (page 30).

STRETCHING THE DOUGH

1. Place the dough in the centre of a large wooden work surface. Use the pin to flatten the ball in the centre, keeping the pin balanced on either side and placing your hands toward the outside of the pin **(A)**. Roll the dough out using a gentle but firm back-and-forth motion. Trust your body - you have an intuitive knowledge of how to roll out the dough.

2. Turn the dough 90 degrees, flatten again in the centre, and roll out using an even back-and-forth motion **(B)**. Your goal is to keep the dough round and the same thickness throughout. (If the dough ends up being too thick in some places, press down with a little more force when rolling to even it out.)

3. If desired, roll with your palms and then up onto the front portion of your forearms **(C)**. Continue rolling, always on one side of the dough (don't turn it over), using a light but firm back-and-forth motion to keep the dough even in thickness.

   Turn the dough 90 degrees and repeat the rolling. Do this several times, thinning gradually each time. If desired, roll using the palms of your hands and then roll up onto the front portion of your forearms.

4. When the dough is rolled out to a thickness of about ¼ inch (6 mm), start stretching it as well as rolling it with the pin **(D)**. To do so, fold the top end of the dough over the rolling pin and press down gently so it adheres. Start rolling the dough up on the pin.

5. With each roll of the pin, place both your hands in the centre of the pin and move your fingers lightly but firmly toward the outside of the pin while moving them up and down, using the same motion as if forming a dough "snake." Your goal is to gently stretch the dough from the centre outward toward the edge of the pin **(E)**.

C

D

E

6 Roll the dough up on the pin, leaving about 2 inches (5 cm) of dough from the bottom edge sticking out **(F)**. Use a sharp, jerking movement to flip the edge over the pin so that it slaps down onto the board, thereby stretching out the edge of dough and making a satisfying sound at the same time. Dust the dough edge with extra flour as necessary to keep it from sticking.

7 While it is still rolled up on the pin, turn the dough 90 degrees and unroll onto the work surface **(G)**. Begin rolling again from the centre upward and from the centre downward. If the dough sheet is too big to fit on the work surface, allow the edge to hang down over the front of the table.

8 Repeat the action of rolling the dough up on the pin, rolling toward your body **(H)**. With each roll of the pin, stretch the dough out sideways **(E)**, then flip the edge over to slap it down and turn 90 degrees. Alternate rolling out with the pin with rolling and stretching the dough.

9 When the dough is quite thin but not yet transparent, start sprinkling it with semolina instead of more flour to keep it from sticking while at the same time encouraging the surface of the dough to be more porous as the grainy semolina is rolled onto the dough sheet **(I)**.

10 The sheet of dough is ready when you can see the grain of the wood through it - about $\frac{1}{16}$ inch (2 mm) thick. Hold it up as shown - you should be able to see your fingers through the dough **(J)**. Once rolled out, place the dough between 2 layers of cotton cloth to gently dry, about 20 minutes, turning over once before cutting as desired. The dough is ready when the surface on both sides is dry like cardboard, but not at all brittle.

11 On the upper right is a sheet of hand-rolled pasta dough with its rough surface; on the lower left the same dough is machine-rolled so that it is thinner and smoother **(K)**.

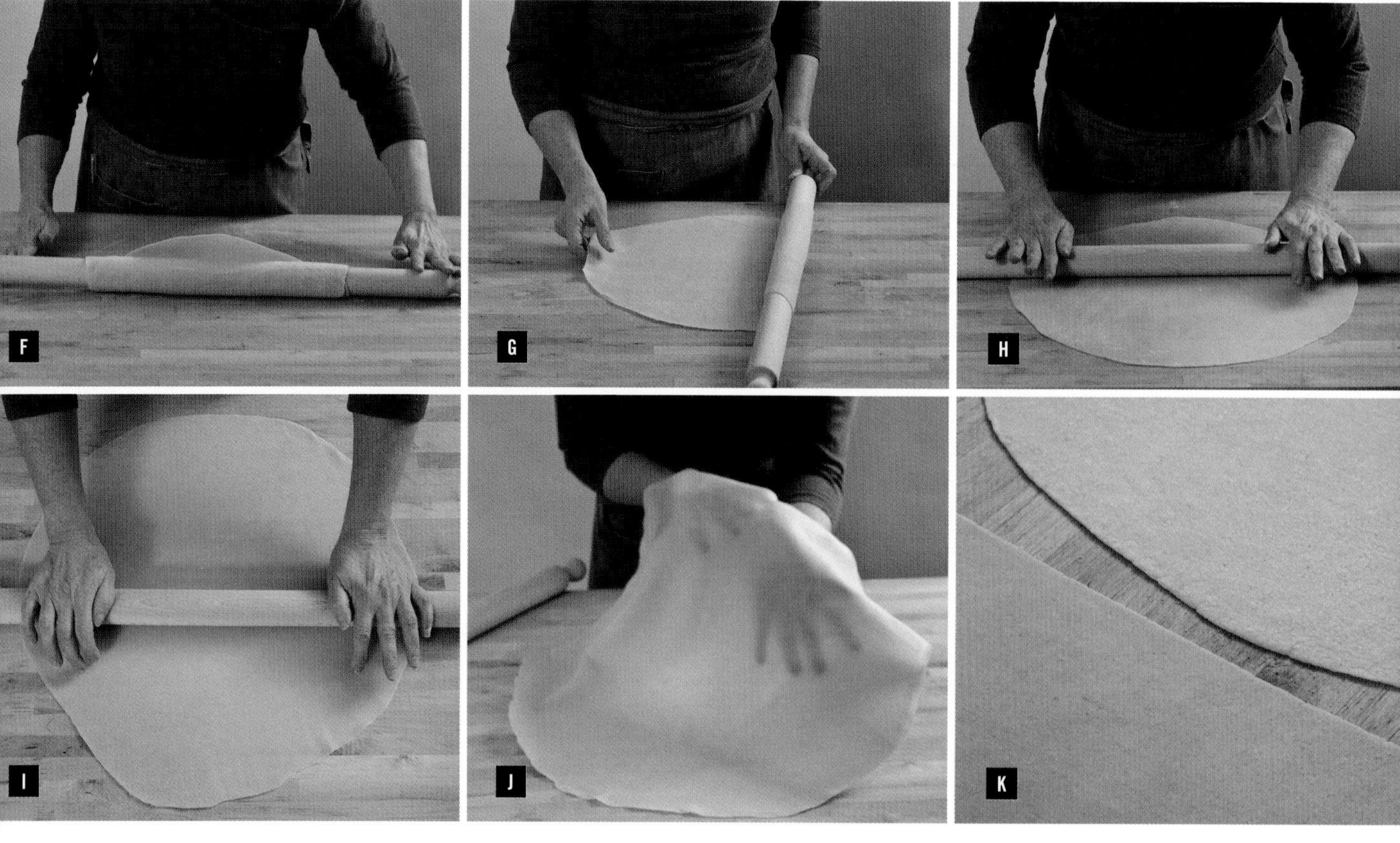

ROLLING PASTA DOUGH WITH A SHEETER

A mechanical pasta sheeter has two steel rollers with a variable opening between the two where the dough is inserted to start the thinning process, as well as a clamp with a large wing nut to attach the board to a worktable. On the far side is a knob to adjust the distance between the two rollers. Opposite it is a handle with a crank to move the dough through the rollers. The same crank is used to crank the dough cutter attachments.

Depending on the brand, the numbers on the knob start at 0 or 1 with the rollers at their maximum distance apart and go up to 6 to 9, with the rollers almost touching. Most often, I roll pasta dough out to number 7 on my Atlas machine; higher than that and the sheets become overly thin and fragile. However, the firmer the dough, the thicker the sheet, so a softer dough such as pierogi (page 148) rolled out to number 7 will be thinner than a dense dough such as whole wheat pasta (page 37) rolled out to the same number.

For stuffed pasta, roll a bit thinner because the dough will be doubled; for sheet or cut pasta strips, cut a little thicker. For specialty hand-shaped pastas such as corzetti, buckwheat pizzoccheri (page 112), and pasta alla chitarra (page 108), roll the dough out thicker, only to about number 4. For delicate doughs such as pierogi and vareniki, roll out a bit thicker so the large amount of filling doesn't burst the dough open when it is cooked.

Here I use Roasted Red Pepper Pasta Dough (page 50) to roll out with the sheeter.

1 For 1 to 1¼ pounds (450 to 565 g) of pasta dough, divide into 4 sections, keeping all but 1 covered to prevent the pasta from forming a hard skin. Using your fingers, flatten out a section of dough by hand into a rough "tongue" shape **(A & B)**. Using a hand-cranked pasta sheeter on number 1 setting (the next-to-the-largest opening between the rollers is usually 1, but some machines start at 1, so it would be 2), begin flattening out the dough.

2 Dust the pasta rectangle lightly with flour, then roll out starting on the next-to-the-largest opening until the dough is tongue-shaped and about 3 times the width of the dough slot **(C)**.

A

B

C

3 Fold in 3 crosswise, dimpling with your fingers so the layers adhere **(C)**. (The object is to get an even piece of dough almost as wide as the rollers.)

4 Go back to number 0 (or 1, depending on the machine) on the pasta sheeter as your dough is now double-thick. Begin feeding the folded dough through the sheeter while cranking smoothly, sprinkling on both sides with extra flour as needed **(D)**.

5 Reduce the thickness of the dough 1 number for each round of rolling until you have obtained the pasta thickness that you desire, supporting the end of the dough with your hands **(E)**. Do not skip any numbers as the action of rolling also kneads the dough.

NOTE: Avoid stopping and starting while cranking: Your pasta sheet will be of uneven thickness.

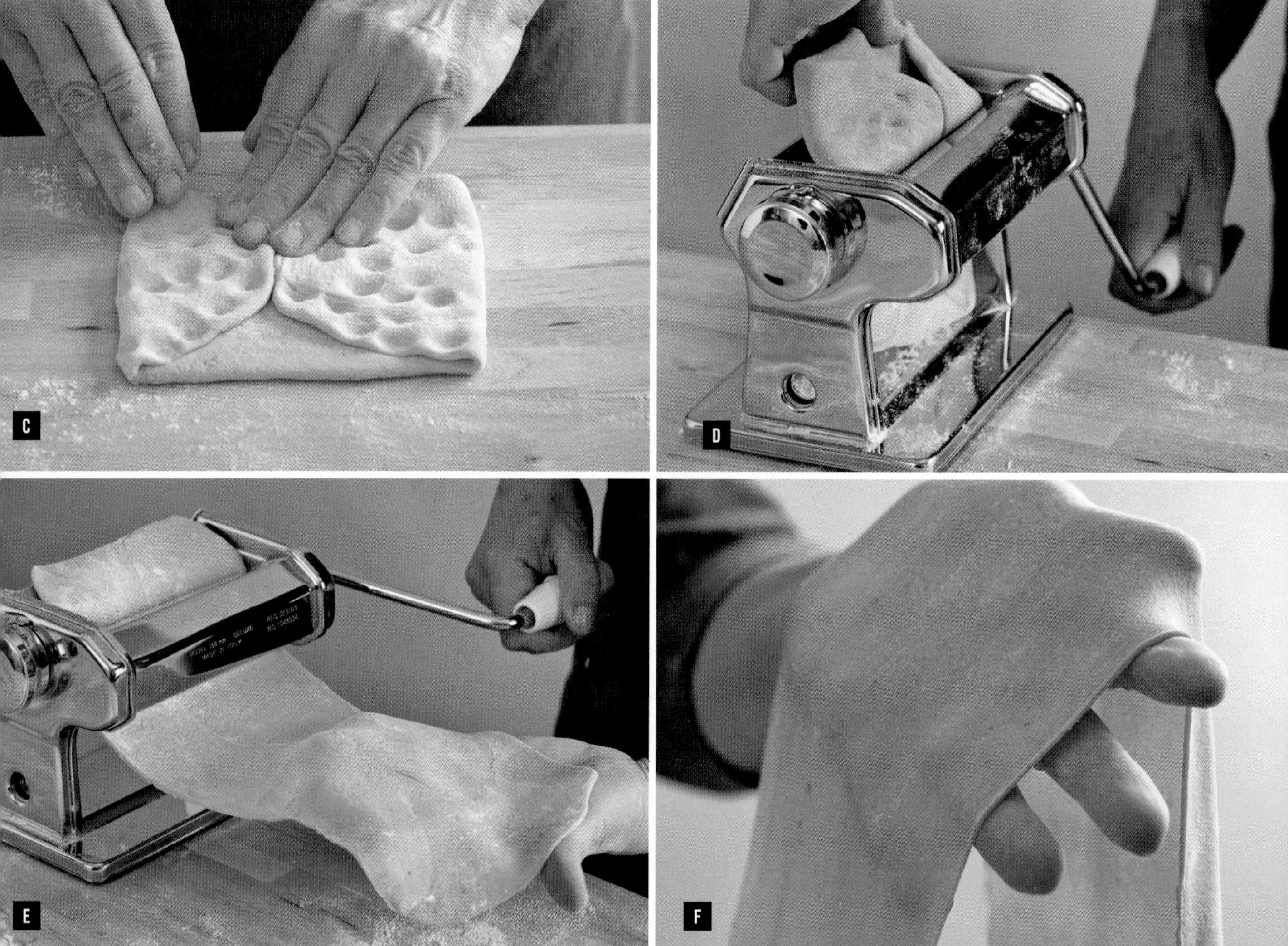

As the dough is rolled out thinner, it may begin to get sticky, especially on the next-to-last and last rounds. Dust with more flour as needed, but don't overdo it. Once the pasta has been fully rolled out, it should be coated by a thin to nonexistent layer of flour. Any excess flour that is not incorporated into the dough will wash off in the cooking water and tend to make gluey pasta.

6 Continue to roll, notching up 1 number each time, until you reach the next-to-the-highest or second-from-highest number, which is almost the smallest opening between the rollers. (Usually the highest setting will yield a too-thin dough, unless the dough you're working with is extremely firm.) The finished dough should be quite thin, but not quite transparent **(F)**. On the Atlas machine I use here, I generally roll out to number 7 (the highest is number 9).

If the dough breaks apart, is irregularly shaped, or sticks to the machine and makes holes, do not worry. Just fold up the sheet of dough into a regular shape that fits the width of the pasta machine. Dust the new piece of dough with flour, and start rolling again following all the above steps.

If the dough is elastic and wants to spring back, push it back into a compact shape, cover, and allow it to rest at room temperature for about 30 minutes to relax the gluten before rolling.

EXTRUDING: ANOTHER WAY TO FORM PASTA

Dry pasta that comes in a box is produced industrially by extrusion. The firm golden dough, made from just durum semolina and water, is forced through a die similar to a meat grinder with a series of openings of various shapes and sizes. It is then cut to length and dried. The best quality dried pasta is extruded through bronze dies, which impart a rough, sandy texture to the surface that better grabs onto slippery sauces and changes the dough surface colour from yellow to ivory. This artisanal-type pasta is dried slowly at a lower temperature to better maintain its inherent flavour and supple texture, and is higher in price. Common commercial pasta is extruded through Teflon or other nonstick surface–coated dies and has a smooth yellow surface. It is dried at a higher temperature for speed but loses some of its flavour and becomes more brittle in the process, though it costs less.

While home extruding machines or attachments are available, the dies are made from plastic, rather than bronze. Because the machines themselves don't have the powerful motors of commercial equipment, the dough must be softer in order to run through the extruder. One exception is the heavy bronze torchio traditionally used to extrude the very stiff dough for Venetian whole wheat bigoli, which resembles thick spaghetti. Along with many other pasta artisans, I do not care for the homogenised texture of most home-extruded pasta.

CHAPTER **THREE**

FLAVOURING PASTA DOUGH

I HAVE BEEN inspired by the creativity of Italian *pastai* (pasta makers) to develop an artist's palette of colourful pasta ever since I came upon a Venetian pasta shop full of fanciful flavoured pastas including artichoke, nettle, porcini mushroom, and asparagus.

Most flavoured pastas are based on vegetable purées, but ingredients such as squid ink, saffron threads, and red wine add colour, texture, and delicate flavour to handmade pasta. The key is to choose ingredients that are intensely coloured, cooked soft enough to be incorporated fully into the dough, and with most of the water either cooked out or squeezed out to concentrate colour and flavour.

Some traditional pasta dough additions include truffles (especially in Umbria), white wine, borage, nettles, and fresh herbs (especially in Liguria), pig's blood (in Trentino), as well as squash and chestnuts, and meat stock and shrimp roe in China. The Sardinian practice of colouring pasta with locally grown saffron to make it appear rich in eggs, is quite old. The dough for the Baroque *vincigrassi* of Le Marche includes Marsala wine. Elsewhere, spices, especially black pepper, nutmeg, cinnamon, and lemon zest, flavour pasta dough and gnocchi.

So, respect and learn from tradition, but use your imagination to perfect your own colourful fresh pasta.

In this chapter, you will learn to make pasta flavoured with roasted red peppers, young green asparagus, baby spinach, red beets, orange squash, concentrated red wine, dried porcini mushrooms, saffron threads, squid ink, lemon zest with black pepper, and chocolate.

Each dough is diverse in colour, texture, and flavour, and all are enhanced by appropriate sauces. Saffron works well with seafood as does squid ink, while porcini and red wine complement hearty meat ragù and

Colourful flavoured pasta doughs from left to right: saffron, beet, spinach, red pepper, asparagus, squid ink, squash, and porcini mushroom.

mushroom sauces. Lemon-pepper pasta especially suits delicate spring vegetables such as snow peas, asparagus, and green onions or even wild ramps and fiddlehead ferns, tender herbs such as chives, basil, and tarragon, and light cream sauces.

This is your opportunity to make a colourful, creative pasta statement, something found only in your own homemade pasta. Try green peas, artichokes, gold beets, and arugula; tangerine zest and juice; young nettles, zucchini (using only the colourful peel); finely ground chili flakes, sun-dried tomato purée, finely chopped black oil-cured olives, or curry powder.

Cook vegetables until tender but brightly coloured, shock by running under cold water, drain, then finely chop or purée to prevent holes in the dough. The amount of addition should be no more than 20 percent of the dough weight.

ROASTED RED PEPPER PASTA DOUGH

THIS IS A COLOURFUL PASTA with a sweet aftertaste and a lovely bright colour that marries best with light vegetable and fresh herb sauces that show off its beauty. Do not cover it with a heavy sauce made from cream or canned tomatoes. The more intensely red the pepper and the redder the paprika, the brighter the dough. (Hot-house peppers are usually the best choice.)

6 ounces (170 g) roasted red pepper (about 1½ large peppers), homemade or purchased
1 tablespoon (7 g) sweet red paprika
¾ pound (350 g) Pasta Flour Mix (page 24)
2 large eggs, at room temperature

Yield: about 18 ounces (500 g), serves 5 to 6

1 Drain the peppers well and pat dry with a paper towel, rubbing off any stray seeds and bits of skin at the same time. (These tend to make holes in the dough when it's rolled.)

Purée the peppers in a blender or food processor then transfer to a small skillet or pot. Cook over medium heat, stirring often, until the pepper purée is thick enough to hold its shape. Cool to room temperature, then mix in the paprika.

2 Pour the flour into a large bowl or onto a work surface, preferably wooden, and shape it into a "volcano" **(A)**. Add the eggs and red pepper purée into the crater.

3 If you are making pasta in a bowl, use a large table fork to begin incorporating the flour, starting with the inner rim and working in the flour from the bottom up **(B)**. Spin the bowl counterclockwise if you're right-handed (clockwise if you're left-handed) while working in the flour with the fork.

If you are making pasta on a board, as more flour gets incorporated, push the flour up on the outside to maintain the crater shape so the egg doesn't run out. If you are right-handed, beat the egg counterclockwise while using your left hand to support the outer wall of the volcano. If you are left-handed, beat the egg clockwise while using your right hand to support the volcano.

A

B

4 If you are making the dough in a bowl, start kneading the dough once the pasta forms large clumps. When all the loose flour has been incorporated and the dough has formed a rough but cohesive mass, about 4 minutes, transfer it to the board to finish kneading **(C)**. (If loose flour remains and resists incorporation into the dough, add 2 to 3 teaspoons water, toss with the loose flour, and incorporate into the dough mass.)

If you are making pasta on a board, continue incorporating flour until it has all been added and the dough forms large clumps. (If loose flour remains and resists incorporation into the dough, add 2 to 3 teaspoons water, toss with the loose flour, and incorporate into the dough mass.) Scrape up and discard any leftover hard bits of dough.

5 Dust the board lightly with flour and begin kneading the dough **(D)**. Use the palms of your hands to knead, pressing down and away from your body, forming the dough into a flattened oval. Fold the top edge over the dough and form it back into a ball. Rotate the dough ball a quarter turn (to the right if you're right-handed and to the left if you're left-handed) and repeat until the dough is cohesive and moderately smooth, about 5 minutes.

If making stuffed pasta, the dough should stick lightly to your fingers but pull away cleanly. For sheet pasta, add enough extra flour to make a firmer dough that releases easily from your fingers.

HOW TO ROAST RED PEPPERS

To roast red peppers, preheat a grill, an electric burner, or a gas burner. Arrange peppers directly on the grill or burner and cook until charred on all sides, turning often so the pepper skin chars evenly without darkening the flesh underneath. Remove from the heat, and rest until cool enough to handle. Rub off skin, rinsing hands occasionally in cold water to remove skin pieces. Remove and discard stem, seeds and white connective tissue. Avoid using water to rinse peppers as this washes off flavour. Store peppers in a covered container for up to 1 week refrigerated.

6 Cover the dough with a bowl or a damp cloth, or wrap in plastic and allow it to rest for 30 minutes at room temperature before rolling or shaping as desired **(E)**. The dough will continue to absorb the flour as it rests. If the dough is sticky after resting, and you're rolling it by machine, you may wish to incorporate more flour by sprinkling the dough when you roll out the pasta to keep it from sticking.

C

D

E

ASPARAGUS PASTA DOUGH

A BEAUTIFUL ASPARAGUS dough is perfect for spring. Look for very thin, intensely green asparagus; large asparagus with white stalks aren't worth using. Use this dough to make the Giant Asparagus Raviolo with Soft-Cooked Egg (page 158). Or, cut the dough into fettuccine, tagliatelle, or pappardelle; dress with butter or extra-virgin olive oil and grated Parmigiano-Reggiano cheese with sautéed asparagus tips, spring onions, and tender herbs such as tarragon, chives, chervil, and marjoram. Don't be tempted to cut off the tips for garnish - while admittedly beautiful, the tips also impart the deepest green colour and most concentrated asparagus flavour to the dough.

½ pound (225 g) thin dark green asparagus
¾ pound (350 g) durum flour
2 large egg yolks

Yield: about 1¼ pounds (565 g), serves 6 to 8

1. Cut off the tougher white bottom 3 to 4 inches (7.5 to 10 cm) of the asparagus stalks and either discard or freeze for vegetable stock. Slice the asparagus into ¼-inch (6-mm) pieces.

2. Bring 1 cup (235 ml) of salted water to a boil in a small skillet or pot and add the asparagus. Bring the water back to a boil over high heat and cook until the asparagus is crisp-tender and brightly coloured, about 2 minutes.

2. Drain, saving the cooking water if desired for vegetable stock. Shock the asparagus under cold water to set the colour, and drain well.

4. Place the asparagus and egg yolks into the work bowl of a food processor and process until the asparagus is in fine bits. Follow the instructions in Roasted Red Pepper Pasta Dough (page 50) to complete.

SPINACH PASTA DOUGH (PASTA VERDE)

THE CLASSIC FLAVOURED pasta is best made with baby spinach leaves because they contain less fibre and mix into the dough better than heavy-ribbed full-grown spinach, which works best for pasta fillings. Some people prefer to pass the cooked spinach through a sieve to remove the fibre, but I like to make streaky green dough that is clearly handmade. Use the smaller amount of flour for a soft dough suitable for stuffing, the larger amount for a firm dough for cut pastas.

6 ounces (170 g) washed baby spinach leaves, stems removed
2 large eggs, at room temperature
10 to 12 ounces (275 to 350 g) Pasta Flour Mix (page 24)

Yield: about 1 pound to 18 ounces (450 to 500 g), serves 4 to 6

1. Fill a small pot with about ½ cup (120 ml) cold water and bring to a boil. Add the spinach and cook until wilted, turning often so the spinach cooks evenly. Cook 1 minute longer or until the spinach is soft but still brightly coloured. Drain (saving the water if desired for vegetable stock) and shock under cold running water to set the colour. Squeeze out most of the water from the spinach and form it into a compact ball. Slice the ball thinly in one direction then turn crosswise and slice again to cut the fibres. Chop finely then place spinach and eggs in the food processor and process until very fine. (If you skip the chopping step, the spinach will be quite stringy.)

2. Follow the instructions in Roasted Red Pepper Pasta Dough (page 50) to complete.

RED BEET PASTA DOUGH

THIS IS A nontraditional but striking dough that pairs well with tangy white cheese including *mozzarella di bufala*, fresh goat cheese, and mascarpone. A little goes a long way - beets contain betanin, the powerful pigment that gives them their intense red colours. Medium beets will impart magenta colour; larger beets will impart a darker, almost purplish colour. Some of the colour will inevitably leach out into the water, but the cooked pasta will still be quite bright.

1 medium red beet
1 tablespoon (15 ml) vinegar
Pinch sea salt
2 large eggs, at room temperature
10 ounces (275 g) Pasta Flour Mix (page 24)

Yield: about 1 pound (450 g), serves 4 to 6

1. Place the beet in a medium pot with a lid and add enough water to cover by about 2 inches (5 cm). Add the vinegar and salt and bring to a boil. Cover and reduce heat and simmer 45 minutes or until the beet is tender when pierced. Cool, then rub off the skin. You'll need only 2 ounces, or 60 g (by weight), or ¼ cup, or 60 ml (by volume), of the beet. (Drained, cooked canned beets will also work though the colour won't be as bright.)

2. Chop the beet and combine with the eggs in the bowl of a food processor. Process until finely ground and only small bits of beet remain.

3. Follow the instructions in Roasted Red Pepper Pasta Dough (page 50) to complete.

SQUASH PASTA DOUGH

SQUASH IS ONE of the more challenging plants to use for pasta dough as the pulp tends to keep exuding the liquid it contains, though the results are quite beautiful and perfect for fall pasta creations. (Some Italian pasta is made using the squash cooking liquid instead of water with the squash itself used as the filling.) Canned pumpkin is easier to use but duller in colour. I recommend dense, hard squash such as pie pumpkin, Japanese kuri, calabaza, or butternut (see note).

½ pound (225 g) diced pie pumpkin or other dense orange squash
¾ pound (350 g) Pasta Flour Mix (page 24)
½ teaspoon ground mace or grated nutmeg, optional
2 large eggs, at room temperature

Yield: about 1¼ pounds (565 g), serves 6 to 8

1. Steam the pumpkin either in a steaming rack placed over boiling water and covered or placed in a microwaveable bowl with about ¼ cup (60 ml) of water and microwaved until tender, about 5 minutes on high. Place the squash in a colander to drain and cool. Squeeze out excess liquid by placing the squash on a strong clean towel, rolling up and then twisting the ends. Chop the squash into small bits - you should have about ½ cup (120 ml) of squash left. (Save the squash juices to add to the pasta dough if it is too dry, or add to the sauce.)

2. Follow the instructions in Roasted Red Pepper Pasta Dough (page 50) to complete.

NOTE: When paring the squash, make sure to remove both the outer layer of skin and the inner waxy layer, leaving only the tender orange-coloured flesh. If using butternut, the "neck" portion is ideal for this pasta as the flesh in this part of the squash is denser and less stringy than the "bulb" portion. The precut cubes of butternut squash sold in the supermarket produce aisle work well and are easy to use.

RED WINE PASTA DOUGH

PASTA MADE FROM this dough works best cut into fettuccine or pappardelle and tossed with hearty wintertime preparations such as red wine–based meat sauces, especially if made with game, wild mushrooms, and chestnuts. I cook the wine until syrupy to concentrate flavour and colour before adding it to the pasta dough. Because the dough is sticky, roll out a bit thicker than normal, to number 6 on an Atlas machine. If you try to roll it thinner, the action will create bubbles in the dough sheets.

1 cup (235 ml) dry red wine, preferably a dark, hearty full-bodied wine such as Syrah or Cabernet
¼ cup (2 large) egg whites, at room temperature
10 ounces (275 g) Italian 00 flour, Korean flour, or unbleached all-purpose flour

Yield: about 1 pound (450 g), serves 4 to 6

1. Place the wine in a small nonaluminum pot and cook down until thick and syrupy and about ½ cup (120 ml) of liquid remains, 6 to 8 minutes. Note that the wine may flame if it's high enough in alcohol. Just allow the flames to burn until they burn out. Cool the wine to room temperature.

2. Follow the instructions in Roasted Red Pepper Pasta Dough (page 50) to complete.

PORCINI MUSHROOM PASTA DOUGH

PORCINI MUSHROOMS, *Boletus edulis*, the "king of mushrooms" in Italy, are large, rich, and meaty. Known as *cèpes* in French and *steinpilz* in German, they have fat, firm, curved, white stalks and broad dark brown caps with a spongy layer of long, miniscule tubes instead of gills beneath the cap. You can grind dried porcini using a clean coffee/spice grinder, making powder with small bits that show up as attractive flecks in the dough. You may also purchase porcini powder, though it won't have the textural interest of porcini you grind yourself.

½ ounce (14 g), or about ¼ cup, dried porcini mushrooms
¾ pound (350 g) Pasta Flour Mix (page 24)
3 large eggs, at room temperature
3 to 4 tablespoons (45 to 60 ml) tepid water
Extra flour for rolling

Yield: about 1¼ pounds (565 g), serves 6 to 8

1. Place the mushrooms in a spice or coffee grinder and grind to a fine powder. (You may do this in the food processor, but it won't be as fine and will need to be passed through a sieve to remove any larger bits of porcini that could make holes in the dough.) You should end up with about ¼ cup (30 g) porcini powder (or use purchased porcini powder).

2. Place the powdered porcini and flour into a large mixing bowl and whisk together to combine well.

3. Follow the instructions in Roasted Red Pepper Pasta Dough (page 50) to complete.

SAFFRON–WHITE WINE PASTA DOUGH

SAFFRON, *Crocus sativus*, is the three orange-red stigmas (also known as pistils) attached to the base of the autumn flowering crocus flower, a member of the Iris family. Saffron has a pungent, earthy, bittersweet flavour with a unique, acrid, haylike aroma. When using saffron for pasta, soak the threads in liquid so their intense colour will disperse evenly. Store saffron, tightly sealed, in the freezer. Iranian and Kashmiri saffron are top quality, with deep orange-red threads. Iran and Spain produce 80 percent of the world's crop.

½ teaspoon saffron threads
¾ cup (175 ml) dry white wine
4 egg yolks
¾ pound (350 g) durum flour

Yield: about 1¼ pounds (565 g), serves 6 to 8

1. Crush the saffron threads in your fingers (make sure they're dry or your hands will be dyed yellow-orange). Place the white wine in a small bowl and add the saffron. Steep the threads about 15 minutes or until the liquid is yellow-orange. Add the egg yolks and whisk to combine.

2. Follow the instructions in Roasted Red Pepper Pasta Dough (page 50) to complete.

SQUID INK
PASTA DOUGH

THIS DRAMATIC BLACK pasta really tastes of the sea and is best complemented by a liquidy seafood sauce. Look for the ink, usually imported from Spain in the United States, from seafood suppliers or specialty stores. Two teaspoons is more than enough for one batch of dough. Anise enhances its flavour.

2 teaspoons or 2 (4 g) packets squid ink
½ cup plus 2 tablespoons (140 ml) tepid water
2 tablespoons (30 ml) Pernod or other anise-flavoured pastis (optional, substitute more water)
¾ pound (350 g) Italian 00 flour or unbleached all-purpose flour

Yield: about 1 pound (450 g), serves 4 to 6

1. Dissolve the ink in the water - it's very thick and gooey and a little goes a long way. Make the volcano of flour in a large bowl. Pour the ink-water mixture into the centre. Using a fork, start incorporating the flour as in the Basic Egg Pasta Dough (page 30). Wrap the dough in plastic wrap and allow it to rest at room temperature for at least 30 minutes before rolling.

2. Follow the instructions in Roasted Red Pepper Pasta Dough (page 50) to complete.

CHOCOLATE PASTA DOUGH

HOW MUCH FUN is it to serve chocolate pasta, actually made with reddish-brown Dutch process cocoa? Though chocolate in Italy is not necessarily sweet - wild boar and oxtails are braised with unsweetened chocolate in Rome - chocolate pasta is usually served as a dessert, topped with ice cream or whipped cream or with fresh berries and chocolate sauce. Try chocolate lasagna layered with sweetened ricotta cheese and serve with a "red sauce" made from raspberries, strawberries, and/or tart red currants. Or toss fettuccine with honey, butter, and brandy and top with grated white chocolate "cheese."

¾ pound (350 g) Pasta Flour Mix (page 24)
2½ tablespoons (28 g) Dutch process cocoa
1 teaspoon ground cinnamon, optional
4 large eggs, at room temperature

Yield: about 1¼ pounds (565 g), serves 6 to 8

1. Place the flour, cocoa, and cinnamon in a large bowl, stir to mix, and form the "volcano." Pour the eggs into the centre and use a fork to start incorporating the flour into the mixture.

2. Follow the instructions in Roasted Red Pepper Pasta Dough (page 50) to complete.

NOTE: This pasta is fragile, so take care when handling cut and dried strips. Roll chocolate dough out slightly thicker than normal. The best way to handle it is to roll the partially dried cut strips into nests. Cut into sheets for lasagne, fettuccine, or pappardelle rather than thinner tagliolini, which will tend to break.

LEMON-PEPPER PASTA DOUGH

THIS SPRIGHTLY PASTA dough is a crowd-pleaser that complements sauces with seafood, vegetables, and chicken. Or, simply dress it with extra-virgin olive oil and grated Parmigiano-Reggiano cheese. A Microplane grater removes just the outer brightly coloured and fragrant zest of the lemon without any of the bitter pith.

¾ pound (350 g) Pasta Flour Mix (page 24), 00 Italian flour, or Korean flour
3 large eggs, at room temperature
Juice of 1 lemon (about 3 tablespoons, or 45 ml)
Grated zest of 3 lemons, preferably organic
2 teaspoons freshly milled black pepper

Yield: about 1¼ pounds (565 g), serves 6 to 8

1. Place the flour in a large bowl and form the "volcano."
2. In a small bowl, combine the eggs, lemon juice, lemon zest, and black pepper.
3. Pour the egg mixture into the centre of the flour and use a fork to start incorporating the flour into the mixture.
4. Follow the instructions in Roasted Red Pepper Pasta Dough (page 50) to complete.

PASTA COOKING TIPS

Fresh egg pasta (whether just made or air-dried) has a different toothsome quality than dried semolina pasta. Fresh egg pasta should be resistant to the bite but still cooked all the way through. Dry semolina pasta should be cooked just until it has a tiny hard core and is still yellow and bouncy.

■ Cook the pasta in plenty of generously salted boiling water using the highest heat possible so that the water returns to a boil as soon as possible. Pasta cooked in water that is not boiling will be gluey and unpleasant to eat.

■ Have the sauce hot and ready to go before the pasta is done. Once the pasta has been cooked and drained (save a little of that starchy pasta water to help bind a thin sauce), transfer either to a warmed (important) large shallow bowl or to a large skillet.

■ Remove the pasta from the water a minute or two before it is done so that it will finish cooking in the sauce, absorbing the sauce and thickening it at the same time.

■ Use a large fork and spoon, two forks, or kitchen tongs (though many chefs frown on these as they tend to break up the pasta) to toss the pasta with the sauce. Separate the strands, lift, toss, and swirl the pasta to coat it. Finish with either a pat of butter or a drizzle of extra-virgin olive oil to add shine and rich mouthfeel. Serve immediately, preferably in heated pasta bowls.

PART II:
THE PASTA

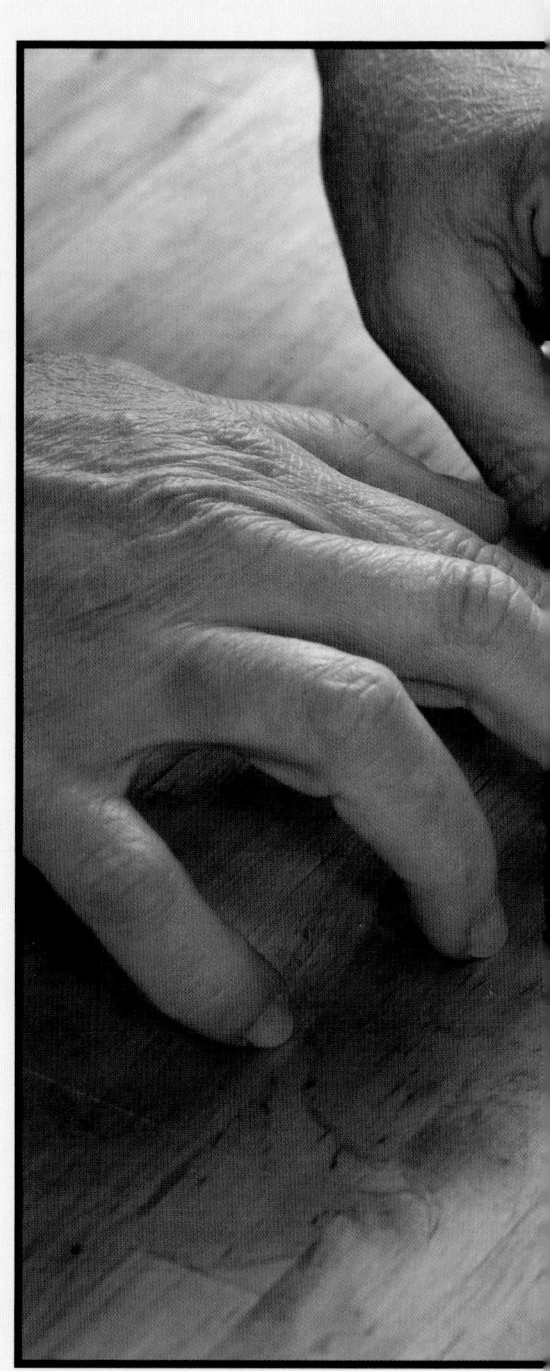

CHAPTER **FOUR**

DUMPLINGS

IN THIS CHAPTER you'll find simple unstuffed dumplings: sweet or savory lumps of dough made from just about any ingredients, including wheat flour, other grains such as cornmeal or rye, potatoes, bread, or crackers. Ground meat, cheese, cooked vegetables, mushrooms, or eggs may be mixed into the dough. Whether known as dumplings or gnocchi, they are the oldest, most primitive form of pasta. Making them light rather than leaden calls for careful attention to proportion and technique.

Gnocchi (pronounced "n-yukky") is the Italian word for dumplings, a plural of *gnocco*, meaning "lump," which derives from a Germanic word for an irregularly shaped knot (as in wood). They are the ancestor of almost all Italian pastas. *Gnochetti* is the diminutive used for smaller dumplings. The first recipes for gnocchi were recorded as far back as the thirteenth century, though their origins are far older. Gnocchi are popular in German-speaking countries as *knaidl* or *knödel*, the term used for the matzo balls traditionally served in chicken soup by Jews of Eastern European background and the equivalent of *canederli* in the formerly Austrian province of Friuli, Italy.

Gnocchi are the ancestor of many types of Italian pasta including Pugliese cavatelli and orecchiette, and Sardinian malloreddus. Potato-based dumplings didn't enter Italian cuisine until the late nineteenth, or even early twentieth, century. One early name for them was *pallottole di patate* (potato bullets). Gnocchi are made from potato, semolina (Roman style), chestnuts, barley, rye, squash, rice, ricotta cheese, spinach, Swiss chard, bread crumbs, bread

Cut potato gnocchi ready to cook

cubes, polenta, or more fanciful ingredients such as wild nettles (*ortiche*), almond paste, raisins, bits of prosciutto, speck (smoked ham), and goose fat. When made with greens and ricotta, they are often known as ravioli gnudi, or naked ravioli, because the filling is not clothed in pasta dough (see page 72).

Some of the gnocchi and related dumplings in this chapter are not technically considered to be in the category of pasta, which consists of dough made from flour mixed with liquid that is firm enough to knead and then roll out and cut into various shapes. Because we eat them in a similar way to pasta, I have included them here.

POTATO GNOCCHI

GOLD-FLESHED POTATOES, such as Yukon gold, give these potato gnocchi an attractive colour. Larger potatoes with thicker skin will have denser flesh that requires less flour to thicken. Russets (baking potatoes) make substantial gnocchi that hold their shape but don't have the buttery flavour of golds. New potatoes or waxy potatoes such as red bliss are not suitable. Some people make potato gnocchi without egg because it makes a lighter, though more difficult to handle, dough. This recipe has just 1 yolk, just enough to bind the dough. If possible, use 00 flour here for the silkiest, lightest gnocchi. Chives add savory oniony flavour and attractive green flecks to the gnocchi.

1 pound (450 g) large yellow potatoes
1 egg yolk
2 tablespoons (6 g) thinly sliced chives (optional)
1 teaspoon fine sea salt
Ground white pepper to taste
¼ pound (115 g) unbleached all-purpose flour, Italian 00 flour, or Korean flour (if using 00 or Korean flour, increase the amount to 5 ounces, or 140 g), plus extra for rolling

Yield: about 1 pound (450 g), serves 4 to 6

Cutting potato gnocchi

1 Steam the potatoes in their skins, or boil them in salted water until tender but not mushy, about 40 minutes. (Don't peel the potatoes before boiling, as they will absorb too much water.) Drain well and cool them just long enough to be able to handle them, then peel the potatoes and put them through a potato ricer or food mill while still hot. Chill the potatoes in the refrigerator. (By chilling the potatoes, you will need less flour to make a dough firm enough to hold its shape when cooked.)

2 In a large bowl or on a wooden work surface as shown, combine the potatoes with the egg yolk, chives, salt, and white pepper.

A

3 Form the potato mixture into a ring and place the flour in the middle. Gently, using only your fingertips while patting and pinching, mix the flour into the potato mix to make a fairly firm mass that doesn't stick to your fingers.

4 Work until just combined, as if you were making a pastry dough **(A)**. The object here is to use the minimum amount of flour and to develop its gluten only enough to stick the whole thing together. Rough handling will result in tough, gluey gnocchi.

TIP: Before shaping all the gnocchi, it's a good idea to test 1 or 2 to make sure the dough is firm enough to hold its shape when cooked. Try cooking a couple in salted boiling water. If they fall apart, which usually happens toward the end of the cooking time, gently pat in an ounce or so (30 g or so) of flour.

5 Throw a little flour onto your work surface and gently roll the dough into a thick sausage shape **(B)**.

6 Using a bench scraper, or a knife with a flat blade, divide the dough into 6 portions **(C)**.

7 Start rolling 1 portion at a time into a "snake," starting from the centre **(D)**. Use an up-and-down motion while moving your hands toward the outside.

B

C

D

8 Roll each snake until it is about the thickness of your index finger and relatively uniform in diameter **(E)**.

9 Dust each rope with flour and then roll again to even out the snakes **(F)**.

10 Cut the dough into pillow-shaped pieces ½ to ¾ inch (1 to 2 cm) long to make individual gnocchi **(G)**.

TO COOK POTATO GNOCCHI:

1 Bring salted water to a boil in a wide, shallow pot. Add the gnocchi, reduce heat to a light rolling boil, and cook the gnocchi until they float to the top. Cook 2 to 3 minutes longer, or until the gnocchi are cooked through but still firm.

2 Skim them from the water using a wire skimmer or slotted spoon. These gnocchi are too fragile to drain in a colander.

3 Toss gently with melted butter and grated cheese or other sauce, such as fresh tomato and shredded basil with small cubes of fresh mozzarella, and serve immediately.

NOTES: If desired, dust each piece lightly with flour and roll up from the cut edge in a C shape along the outside tines of a dinner fork to form ridged gnocchi. Or, roll up on a grater using the cross-cut side. Or, roll up on a ridged wooden gnocchi or garganelli board (see page 122). Set aside on a board dusted lightly with semolina or cornmeal without touching.

It is best to cook the gnocchi as soon as they are formed, as they will become sticky and soft as the flour is absorbed into the dough. Alternatively, freeze the gnocchi following the instructions on page 40. Do not defrost before cooking.

E

F

G

SEMOLINA GNOCCHI (GNOCCHI ALLA ROMANA)

IN ROME, Thursdays are the day when many restaurants and home cooks serve gnocchi in this style, a local specialty. The traditional presentation is to layer the circles of pasta in overlapping rings into a dome shape. Here, they are in a single layer for better browning. In Sardinia, semolina gnocchi are known as *pillas* and are sauced with meat ragù and grated pecorino Sardo and browned in the oven.

A

3½ cups (825 ml) whole milk
1 teaspoon fine sea salt
½ teaspoon freshly grated nutmeg
½ pound (225 g) semolina
1 large egg, at room temperature
2 egg yolks
2 ounces (55 g), or about ¾ cup, grated Parmigiano-Reggiano cheese or Grana Padano cheese, plus extra for sprinkling on top
6 tablespoons (85 g) unsalted butter, softened

SPECIAL EQUIPMENT: 2-inch (5-cm) round cookie cutter; 2-quart (1.9-L) shallow baking dish or gratin dish

Yield: about forty 2-inch (5-cm) gnocchi, serves 6 to 8

B

1 Bring milk with salt and nutmeg to a simmer in a 2- to 3-quart (1.9- to 2.8-L) heavy saucepan (not aluminum, which will discolour the mix) over moderately low heat. Add semolina in a slow stream while constantly stirring to prevent lumps **(A)**.

2 Reduce heat and simmer, stirring constantly with a wooden spoon or a heavy whisk until the mixture begins to pull away from the sides of the pan, about 5 minutes (mixture will be very stiff) **(B)**.

C

3 Remove from heat, cool slightly, then beat in eggs and yolks **(C)**. Beat in ½ cup (50 g) of the cheese and 3 tablespoons (45 g) of the butter, and stir or whisk until mixture is smooth.

D

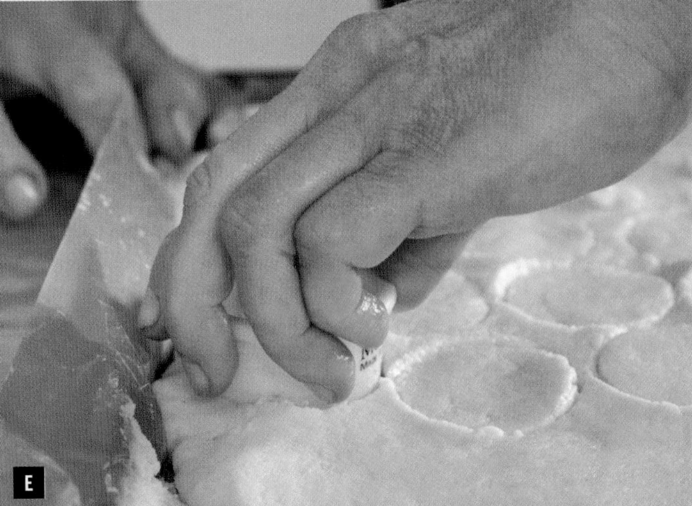
E

F

4 Spread gnocchi mixture into a ½-inch (1-cm)–thick slab on an oiled or parchment paper–lined baking sheet using a lightly oiled silicone spatula **(D)**. Press plastic wrap or parchment paper over top and smooth the top with the palms of your hands. Chill until cold and firm, about 1 hour. This amount fills a 10 x 15-inch (25 x 38-cm) jelly-roll pan perfectly.

5 Preheat the oven to 450°F (230°C, or gas mark 8). Rub a medium shallow baking dish (or a French gratin dish) with 1 tablespoon (15 g) of butter.

6 Have ready a bowl of cold water. Cut out "coins" from gnocchi mixture using a 2-inch (5-cm) ridged or plain round cookie cutter **(E)**. Rinse the cutter in water after each cut. Reserve the scraps. At the end, gather all the scraps together and push them together to form another small ½-inch (1-cm)–thick slab and cut out more coins.

7 Gently transfer the coins (they will be soft), to the baking dish, overlapping them slightly **(F)**. Sprinkle with the remaining cheese and dot with the remaining butter. (You may cover and refrigerate the gnocchi up to 2 days before baking. Allow 40 minutes for baking.)

8 Bake the gnocchi in the upper third of the oven 25 minutes, or until the gnocchi are slightly puffed and lightly browned. If desired, place under a preheated broiler for 2 minutes to brown the top, standing by to make sure the tops don't burn. Let the gnocchi stand 5 minutes to firm up before serving.

RAVIOLI GNUDI

THESE "NUDE" DUMPLINGS aren't made with dough at all, just the naked filling thickened with flour. Like so many pasta dishes, these gnocchi started out as a food of the poor, in this case the peasants of Tuscany, who made them from the limited ingredients they could grow or produce themselves: spinach or Swiss chard, ricotta and aged pecorino (sheep's milk) cheese. They have also been known since at least the fifteenth century as *strozzapreti*, which means "priest stranglers," because they are so delicious the priest would gobble them up.

Salt
1 package (5 ounces, or 140 g) baby arugula (substitute baby spinach)
1 container (15 ounces, or 425 g) or 1 pound (450 g) fresh thick whole milk ricotta, sheep's milk ricotta if necessary
2 large eggs, at room temperature
3 ounces (85 g), or about 1¼ cups, grated Parmigiano-Reggiano cheese, Grana Padano, or aged Pecorino Toscano, plus extra for serving
Freshly ground black pepper and nutmeg
3 ounces (85 g), or about ¾ cup, Italian 00 flour, Korean flour, or unbleached all-purpose flour, plus extra as needed
3 tablespoons (45 g) unsalted butter

Yield: about 36 ravioli gnudi, serves 6

A

B

1 Bring a large wide pot of salted water to a boil. (I use a 6-quart, or 5.7-L, Dutch oven.) Reduce to a simmer, cover, and reserve.

2 Set aside about 1 cup (20 g) of arugula for the garnish. Wilt the remaining arugula either in a small amount of boiling water or sprinkle with a little water and microwave. Immediately run under cold water to set the colour.

3 Squeeze out the excess water and form into a compact ball. Slice thinly in one direction and then slice crosswise to cut the strings. Chop finely.

4 In a large bowl, combine the arugula, ricotta, eggs and cheese and season generously with salt, pepper, and nutmeg. Add about ½ cup (60 g) flour and stir to combine. Add more flour until the mixture forms a soft dough that holds its shape and lightly pulls away from the side of the work bowl.

5 Test if the batter will hold its shape: Scoop up 2 to 3 teaspoons of dough with 1 spoon. Use a second spoon to scrape the dough off the spoon while forming it into a rounded shape, and drop into the boiling water **(A)**. If it falls apart, add only the minimum flour needed to bind the mixture so that the ravioli gnudi stay tender.

6 Drop the ricotta mixture by the rounded teaspoon into the boiling water, making about 36 gnocchi. Bring the water back to a boil, then reduce the heat to a moderate boil and cook the ravioli about 3 minutes, or until they are tender to the core. (Check by cutting one open - you should see little to no dense, uncooked dough in the centre.)

7 The ravioli will puff up and rise to the surface **(B)**. (If any continue to stick to the bottom of the pot, use a wooden spoon or silicone spatula to gently release them.) Allow the ravioli to poach about 6 minutes, or until light and cooked through. Use a Chinese brass wire skimmer or large slotted spoon to gently scoop the ravioli from the water **(C)**. (The ravioli are too fragile to drain in a colander.)

8 Transfer to a large skillet. Over medium heat, melt the butter until it browns and smells nutty. Add the reserved arugula leaves and toss to sizzle. Gently add the cooked and drained ravioli. Use a silicone spatula to turn the ravioli over and coat them with the butter sauce **(D)**. Taste and adjust the seasoning, and serve immediately.

C

D

MATZO BALLS

MATZO BALLS, known as *knaidlach* in Yiddish and *canederli* in Italian, are traditional Ashkenazi (Central and Eastern Europe Jewish) dumplings made from matzo meal, eggs, and often, a bit of onion and ground ginger, shaped by hand, and poached in either salted water or chicken soup. Enriching the dough with chicken schmaltz (rendered chicken fat or the fat skimmed from the top of a pot of chicken soup) or goose fat gives them authentic flavour. Matzo balls may be either "sinkers" or "floaters," depending on the density of the batter, and are invariably served in a steaming bowl of chicken soup. These are in between.

4 large eggs, separated
¼ cup (60 ml) cold chicken stock
¼ cup (60 ml) chicken fat, goose fat, or shortening, melted and cooled
½ cup (80 g) finely diced onion
Generous amount of kosher salt and ground white pepper
½ teaspoon ground ginger
1 to 1½ cups (130 to 195 g) matzo meal

Yield: about 24 matzo balls, serves 8 to 12

1. In a large bowl, whisk together the egg yolks, chicken stock, chicken fat, onion, and salt and pepper. Beat in 1 cup (130 g) of the matzo meal.

2. Separately, beat the egg whites until soft and fluffy but glossy and firm enough to stick to the sides of the bowl. Fold the egg whites into the matzo meal mix in thirds, so as not to deflate **(A)**.

3. The dough is ready when a few streaks of egg white remain **(B)**.

A

B

C

4 Add a little chicken stock or water if the mixture is too stiff; add the remaining matzo meal if it is too thin. The dough should be firm enough to hold its shape well but still slightly sticky. The mixture will stiffen as it sets and chills.

5 Cover and chill the mixture until firm, about 1 hour. Form into walnut-size balls and arrange on a tray lined with wax or parchment paper **(C)**. Bring the chicken soup to a boil in a large wide pot.

6 Dip your hands lightly in water and roll each scooped ball to make it round **(D)**.

7 Place the rounded matzo balls back on the tray until you're ready to cook them **(E)**. Cover with plastic wrap or a damp towel and refrigerate up to 1 day before cooking.

8 Drop the matzo balls one by one into the boiling chicken soup so they don't stick together **(F)**.

9 Boil until the matzo balls float to the top, 3 to 5 minutes. Reduce the heat to a simmer and continue to cook the matzo balls about 10 minutes longer, or until they are cooked all the way through. (Cut one in half to check if the centre is cooked.)

10 Serve immediately, allowing 2 or 3 matzo balls per portion.

TIP: Scoop the matzo balls or other soft dumplings with an ice cream scoop, known as a "disher," for speed and consistent size. (Size 40, meaning 40 portions to the quart, or 44 to the liter, is perfect.) Note that dishers with a side thumb tab are not suitable for left-handers; look for the universal type where you squeeze the sides together instead.

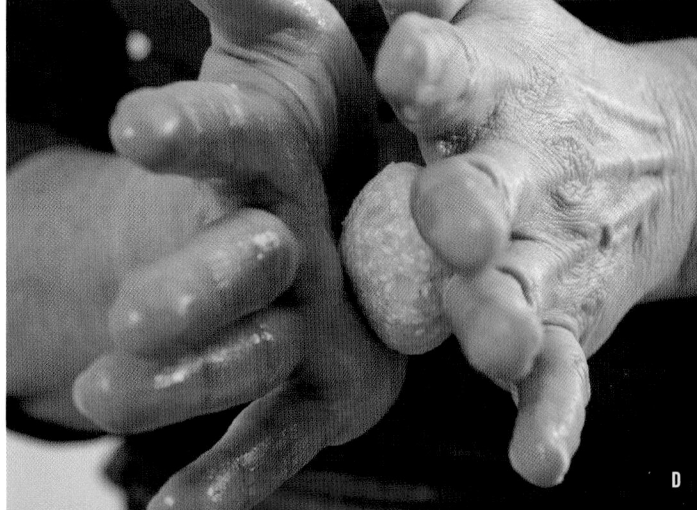
D

E

F

SPAETZLE

SPAETZLE ARE soft dumplings originating in Germany and known throughout the former Austro-Hungarian Empire. They are made from a batterlike soft dough and formed with a special utensil, a spaetzle maker, which looks like a grater topped with a movable box. Like gnocchi, spaetzle can include everything from chestnut flour to spinach, pumpkin, and chickpea flour. Here we use chickpea flour for nutty flavour and light texture, but you may substitute all-wheat flour. Spaetzle can be made ahead and then browned in butter just before serving.

10 ounces (275 g) unbleached all-purpose flour, divided
½ pound (225 g) chickpea flour
2 teaspoons fine sea salt, divided
½ teaspoon freshly grated nutmeg
3 large eggs, at room temperature
2 cups (475 ml) milk
¼ cup (55 g) unsalted butter
1 cup (50 g) soft bread crumbs
¼ cup (15 g) chopped Italian parsley leaves

Yield: about 24 ounces (680 g), serves 8 to 10

1 Combine ½ pound (225 g) of the all-purpose flour, chickpea flour, 1 teaspoon salt, and nutmeg in a large mixing bowl. Whisk together the eggs and milk in a large bowl. Beat the egg mixture slowly into the flour mixture. When the mixture is smooth, whisk in the remaining flour **(A)**.

The dough should be smooth with a consistency halfway between a pancake batter and a dough **(B)**. Cover and allow the dough to rest at room temperature for 30 minutes to relax the gluten.

2 Bring water to a boil in a large wide pot with the remaining teaspoon of salt. Working in batches, press the dough through the holes of a spaetzle maker or a colander directly into the boiling water **(C)**. Stir gently to prevent sticking.

The spaetzle are ready when they float to the surface, about 5 minutes. Remove with a slotted spoon and drain.

3 To finish, melt the butter in a pan over medium heat. Add the bread crumbs and cook until evenly toasted, stirring frequently. Toss the spaetzle with the toasted crumbs and parsley. (If desired, add 1 teaspoon ground caraway or 2 teaspoons whole caraway seed to the butter when browning. Substitute chives for parsley for a delicate oniony flavour.)

LITTLE SPARROWS

Most sources say that their name is a diminutive of *spatz*, or sparrow, so spaetzle means "little sparrows." Others posit that their name derives from the Italian *spezzare*, to break into pieces.

A

B

C

PASSATELLI

A SPECIALTY OF Emilia-Romagna, Le Marche, and Umbria, this unusual dumpling dough, related in concept to spaetzle, is made from dry bread crumbs, Parmigiano-Reggiano cheese, eggs, and beef marrow with nutmeg, black pepper, and lemon zest. Traditionally, the firm dough is pushed through a special bronze extruder or a simpler perforated convex disc with two handles attached on either side, forming small round tubes. Here, we use an Italian potato ricer/passatelli maker fitted with a large-holed removable plate. The passatelli "noodles" drop right into homemade broth to cook.

¼ pound (115 g) finely grated Parmigiano-Reggiano cheese
¼ pound (115 g) fine, dry white bread crumbs (without any brown crust)
1 ounce (28 g) rendered veal or beef marrow, or butter, or a combination
Grated zest of ½ lemon
½ teaspoon sea salt
3 large eggs, at room temperature
2 egg yolks
2 tablespoons (8 g) finely chopped Italian parsley
½ teaspoon fresh grated nutmeg
3 quarts (2.75 L) rich chicken, beef, or capon broth

Yield: 14 ounces (400 g), serves 8 to 10

1. Combine the cheese, crumbs, marrow, lemon zest, salt, eggs, yolks, and parsley well in a large bowl. Grate the nutmeg over top.

2. Whisk all ingredients together to combine **(A)**.

3. Mix the dough with your hands until it is homogenous **(B)**.

4. The dough must be firm enough to hold its shape and just slightly sticky **(C)**. Cover and chill the dough at least 1 hour or until firm. Meanwhile, bring the broth to a boil in a large wide pot, salting to taste. Test the dough by dropping small balls of the dough into the broth. (Add ½ to 1 egg white if the dough is crumbly; add more bread crumbs if it is too soft.)

5. Fit a potato ricer or food mill with a large-holed disc. Press the dough through the holes using firm but even pressure, dropping the passatelli into the boiling broth **(D)**.

A

B

C

6 Use a knife or a bench scraper to cut any remaining passatelli off the ricer, allowing them to drop into the boiling broth **(E)**. Reduce the heat to a slow boil, and cook the passatelli 2 to 3 minutes, or until light and fluffy. Repeat until all the dough has been pressed.

Taste for seasoning, then ladle into serving bowls and garnish with chopped Italian parsley if desired. Serve immediately.

NOTE: If making a larger amount of passatelli, prepare several baking trays lined with parchment or waxed paper. Short lengths of dough will appear through the holes. Allow them to drop off onto the baking trays. Alternatively, press the dough through a meat grinder fitted with a coarse disc.

D

E

CHAPTER **FIVE**

PASTA SHEETS

THE MAJORITY OF handmade pasta is based on *sfoglia*, sheets of dough rolled out by hand using a great, long rolling pin or rolled out by machine using a pasta sheeter. The Italian word *sfoglia* (related to "foil" in English and "feuille" - leaf - in French) refers to the rolled-out sheets of fresh pasta in this chapter.

In Bologna, pasta specialists, skilled women known as *sfogline*, roll out a tablecloth-size sheet of fresh dough with nary a hole or tear. These women use oak rolling pins as long as their arm span; a sheet of hand-rolled dough can only be as large as the length of the pin. The surface of hand-stretched dough is covered with a fine network of stretched gluten strands that give the sauce something to grab onto.

It would take most of a lifetime to reach the level of skill of those pasta masters, but it's easy to use a pasta machine to roll out sheets for the laminated parsley pasta, lasagna, and cannelloni in this chapter. You may also use Hand-Stretched Pasta Dough (page 42).

COMPARING PASTA SHEETS AND **COMMERCIAL EXTRUDED PASTA**

Aside from homemade pasta being completely customizable and versatile, many qualities make sheet pasta distinct from commercial dried extruded pasta (such as spaghetti and ziti).

- When making sheet pasta, you can control the thickness of rolled pasta. You may prefer delicate pasta rolled thin enough to see through or more substantial thicker pasta depending on its use.
- Sheet pasta is thinner than most extruded pasta, so a portion weighs less and is better able to absorb sauces.
- Sheet pasta generally cooks in less than half the time that it takes for extruded pasta.

■ Because of the egg in most fresh dough, sheet pastas work best with meat and poultry sauces, rich cheeses, cream, and butter. Extruded pastas work best with seafood sauces, vegetables, sauces containing sharp condiments such as capers and olives, and simple olive oil–based sauces where cheese is used as a seasoning.

■ Olive oil is the condiment of choice for extruded pasta and butter for fresh-rolled pasta, though olive oil is also delicious and common, especially south of Emilia and in Liguria.

■ Lasagna made with sheet pasta contains multiple thin layers of filling that marry with the pasta to make a unified whole. Lasagna made with thicker extruded pasta (those wide ruffled strips) contain layers of chunky sauce that tend to stay separate and keep their individual character.

HOW TO CARE FOR YOUR PASTA SHEETER

■ Never wash the pasta sheeter, and especially never run it in the dishwasher.

■ Keep the sheeter and all attachments dry to prevent rust.

■ After making pasta dough, brush flour off the machine, rollers, and cutters.

■ Use a plastic scraper to remove any dough. If any stubborn bits of dough remain, allow them to dry out for several days and then scrape again.

■ To lubricate a squeaky pasta sheeter, place a drop of mineral oil where each roller meets the body.

■ Store the pasta sheeter, preferably in its original box, in a dry place.

MALTAGLIATI

IN EMILIA-ROMAGNA, a large sheet of *sfoglia* (or fresh egg pasta) is irregularly cut straight, on the bias, or at odd angles to make this "badly cut" pasta. They are also made from the scraps left after cutting tagliatelle or ravioli. Maltagliati are found all over Italy but especially in Emilia-Romagna, Lombardy, the Veneto, and Le Marche. Large pieces were nicknamed *spruzzamusi* (face sprayers) because that is what would happen when eaten in soup. In Liguria, the dough often contains cheese. In Piedmont, they are known as *foglie di salice* (willow leaves) and are served in bean soup.

MALTAGLIATI IN PUGLIA

To make maltagliati in the style of Puglia, cut a sheet of fresh egg pasta dough into long strips about 2 inches (5 cm) wide. Cut across each strip at varying angles to form short irregularly shaped pieces of dough.

If you have trimmings left over after cutting pasta sheets or strips, make maltagliati by cutting the dough into rough triangles.

1 batch Basic Egg Pasta Dough by Hand (page 30)
Extra flour for rolling

Yield: about 11 ounces (300 g), serves 3 to 4

1. Roll out the dough into a large thin sheet, following the instructions for Hand-Stretched Pasta Dough (page 42). Trim the edges to make a rough rectangle.

2. Dust the sheet with flour and fold into thirds **(A)**.

3. Cut a triangular corner out of each side of the dough. Cut straight across the dough to form another triangle **(B)**. Repeat, cutting corner and centre triangles, until the dough has all been cut.

4. Unfold the pieces as they are cut. Arrange on a mesh pasta drying rack and allow the maltagliati to dry. Or, cook immediately.

A

B

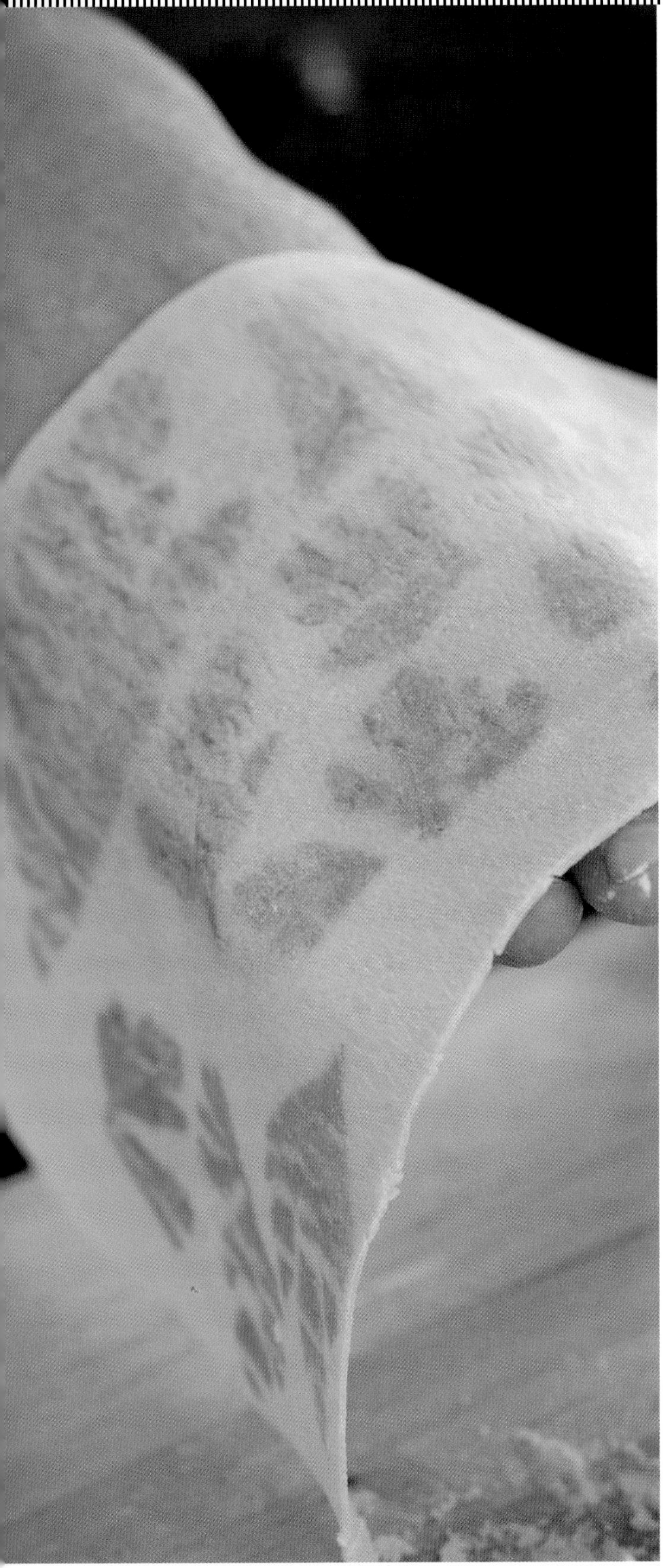

LAMINATED PARSLEY PASTA

THIS ARTFUL DOUGH is laminated, meaning that it is made from sheets of dough pressed together. Here, two sheets of egg dough are layered with fresh Italian parsley leaves, placed close to each other and all facing up. When the layers are joined by rolling them through the pasta sheeter, the leaves are stretched into abstract green shapes, forming a single sheet of dough that resembles handmade paper.

1¼ pounds (565 g) Basic Egg Pasta Dough (for Machine Rolling) (page 30)
Extra flour for rolling
1 large bunch Italian parsley, leaves picked, washed and dried well

Yield: 1¼ pounds (565 g), serves 4 to 6, serves 8 to 10 as soup noodles

1. Roll out the dough, which should be on the moist side, as thin as possible. Cut the sheet in half crosswise. Place one half on a wooden work surface that has been dusted with flour.

2. Arrange the parsley leaves as close as possible to each other without touching over top of the dough **(A)**. (The leaves should be slightly damp so they'll adhere to the pasta. If not, mist the sheet very lightly with water then press the parsley leaves down.)

3. Carefully lay the unfloured side of the second half of the pasta sheet over top and press down all over using your fingertips so that the 2 sheets join together.

4. Adjust the opening so it's one number wider to allow for the double thickness of the dough. Dust the top and bottom layers lightly with flour, then roll again in the pasta sheeter to laminate the sheets, forming a single sheet with parsley leaves enclosed. Note that the parsley will stretch out as well as the dough **(B)**.

5. Cook and serve immediately or dry the pasta sheets on a mesh pasta drying rack then cut into large squares **(C)**.

6. To show off its beauty, this pasta is best served in clear soup broth or with a simple sauce of sage leaves sizzled in brown butter drizzled over top then sprinkled with grated Parmigiano-Reggiano cheese.

B

C

LASAGNA

LASAGNA IS ONE of the earliest known pastas of Italy, and its name derives from the Greek *lasanon*, meaning "tripod" or "kitchen pot." Today, lasagna is made with wheat flour, but other flours were used in the past, including farro (emmer wheat), rye, chestnut, and later, corn. Shapes for lasagna noodles range from squares to wide strips. In Italy's north, lasagna is usually created from dough sheets made from soft wheat flour and eggs; in the south, the dough, usually cut into wide strips and ruffled, is industrially produced from durum flour and water.

Every region of Italy has its own version, but its most famous rendition is Lasagna Bolognese: paper-thin sheets of egg-rich spinach pasta layered with besciamella (cream sauce), ragù (meat sauce), and Parmigiano-Reggiano. Some cooks substitute ricotta for the besciamella for lightness.

ONANO LENTIL LASAGNA

This hearty vegetarian lasagna is a specialty of the small town of Onano in Lazio. Common green or brown lentils tend to disintegrate and taste mealy when cooked. I recommend Italian green lentils from Onano or the better-known Castelluccio lentils, or the small Le Puy lentils or French green lentils. Use either Basic Egg Pasta Dough (page 30), which will be more tender, or Semolina Pasta Dough (page 39), which will have more bite when baked.

Yield: serves 12 to 16

BRAISED GREEN LENTILS

1 quart (950 ml) vegetable stock, or 1 quart (950 ml) water, 1 whole peeled onion, 2 strips lemon zest cut with a potato peeler, 2 bay leaves, and 3 or 4 sprigs thyme tied with kitchen string
1 pound (450 g), or about 2 cups, Italian or French green lentils
Kosher salt and freshly ground black pepper to taste
6 cups (1.4 L) tomato sauce (homemade or purchased)

Yield: 2 quarts (1.9 L)

1 In a 4- to 6-quart (3.8- to 5.7-L) heavy-bottomed pot with a lid, bring the vegetable stock to a boil, add the lentils, and bring back to a boil. Or, bring the water and aromatics to a boil, simmer 20 minutes, then add the lentils and bring back to a boil.

2 Reduce heat to a simmer, skimming off any white foam impurities, then cover and simmer until lentils are half-cooked, about 30 minutes. Season with salt and pepper, cover and cook 20 minutes longer, or until lentils are tender but still firm. (Remove and discard the onion, bay leaves, lemon zest, and thyme sprigs, if using.)

3 Add the tomato sauce then bring the mixture back to a boil over medium heat, stirring occasionally with a wooden spoon or spatula to avoid breaking up the lentils. Reduce heat and simmer until the sauce is thick, about 20 minutes, stirring occasionally. Allow lentils to cool to room temperature. Reserve.

TIP: The lentils can be prepared up to 3 days ahead and refrigerated. They freeze quite well. Warm slightly before using to make it easier to spread them in an even layer.

BESCIAMELLA SAUCE AND PASTA

4 tablespoons (55 g) unsalted butter, plus additional to finish sauce
½ cup (80 g) finely diced onion
Pinch ground cloves
¼ teaspoon dried thyme leaves
6 tablespoons (60 g) all-purpose flour
1 quart (950 ml) milk, scalded
1 cup (235 ml) heavy cream, scalded
½ pound (225 g) imported Italian fontina cheese, frozen and then shredded, or substitute other rich melting cheese such as Taleggio or Bel Paese
¼ pound (115 g) Parmigiano-Reggiano cheese or a mix with pecorino Romano
Kosher salt, freshly ground black pepper, grated nutmeg, and cayenne to taste
1½ pounds (675 g) Basic Egg Pasta Dough (page 30) or Semolina Pasta Dough (page 39)
Extra flour for rolling

Yield: about 5 cups (1.2 L)

PREPARE THE SAUCE:

1 In a medium-size, heavy-bottomed pot, melt the butter, add the onions, cloves, and thyme and cook together until the onions are transparent but not browned. Stir in the flour and cook together until the flour is very lightly browned. Pour in the scalded milk and cream and whisk together vigorously. (Avoid using an aluminum pot, which will discolour the sauce. If that's all you have, stir only with a wooden spoon or silicone spatula, which won't scrape the sides of the pot.)

2 Bring sauce to a boil, simmer for about 15 minutes, stirring often, especially at the corners of the pan where the sauce tends to stick, and then remove from heat. Stir in most of the 2 cheeses, saving a handful of each to sprinkle over top. Season to taste with salt, pepper, nutmeg, and a pinch of cayenne. Cool the sauce, and dot with bits of butter, which will melt and prevent formation of a skin. It's best to work with the sauce at room temperature or slightly warm so it's pourable.

ASSEMBLE THE LASAGNA:

3 Preheat the oven to 375°F (190°C, or gas mark 5). Roll out the pasta dough into sheets slightly thicker than for cut pasta strips (usually number 5 on an Atlas machine) because you will be cooking it twice. Cut each sheet into 2 or 3 smaller sheets. (Here we've used a combination of Basic Egg and All-Yolk pasta that has been hand-stretched.)

4 In a large wide pot, such as a 6-quart (5.7-L) enameled cast-iron Dutch oven, bring salted water to a boil. Working in 3 or 4 batches, gently lay the individual sheets of pasta into the water, boiling only until half-cooked and stirring occasionally with a wooden spoon or silicone spatula to keep them from sticking.

5 Scoop the sheets from the water using a large wire skimmer. Drain the sheets in a colander and rinse under cold water to remove the surface starch, then drain again. Lay out the half-cooked pasta on clean kitchen towels, overlapping as little as possible. Assemble lasagna very soon after cooking, because the sheets will start to stick to the towel as they drain and dry.

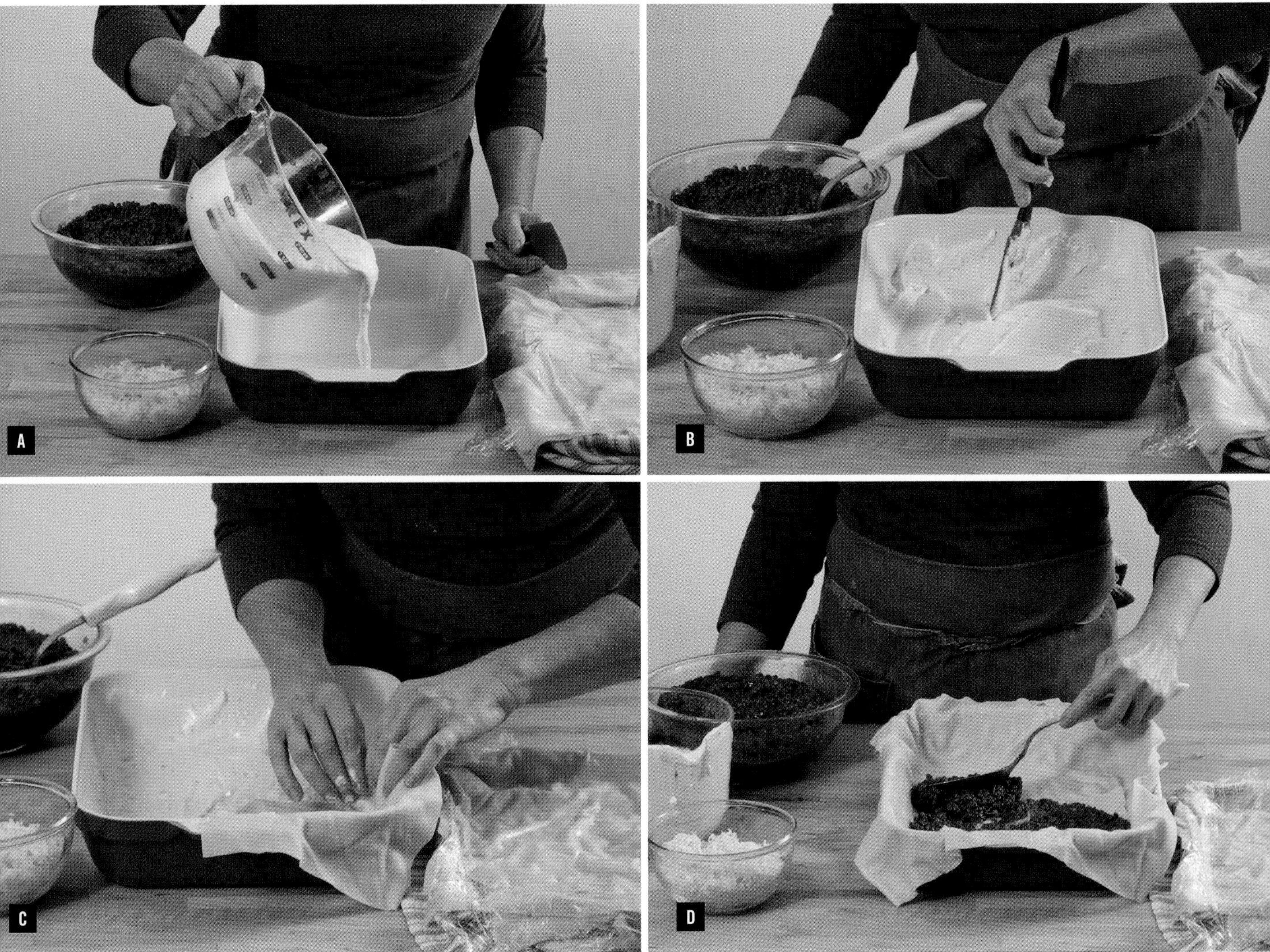

6 Pour a thin layer of besciamella sauce on the bottom of a large lasagna pan **(A)**. Here the pan measures 12 x 8 inches (30 x 20 cm) on the bottom and holds about 6 quarts (5.7 L).

7 Smooth the sauce over the bottom and sides of the pan with a wooden spoon or silicone spatula **(B)**.

8 Cover with a layer of slightly overlapping pasta sheets, overlapping the edge of the pan by several inches (5 to 8 cm) all around **(C)**.

9 Spread one-third of the lentil mixture over top **(D)**.

10 Cover with another layer of pasta, trimmed to fit the inner dimensions of the pan **(E)**. Top with a thin layer of besciamella sauce.

11 Continue layering until all the pasta and filling has been used or the pan is full, whichever comes first **(F)**.

12 Fold the overhanging edges over onto the pan and trim the excess dough. Scissors will make it easier but a small knife will do **(G)**.

13 Wet your hands, then smooth the top with your hands to even it out **(H)**.

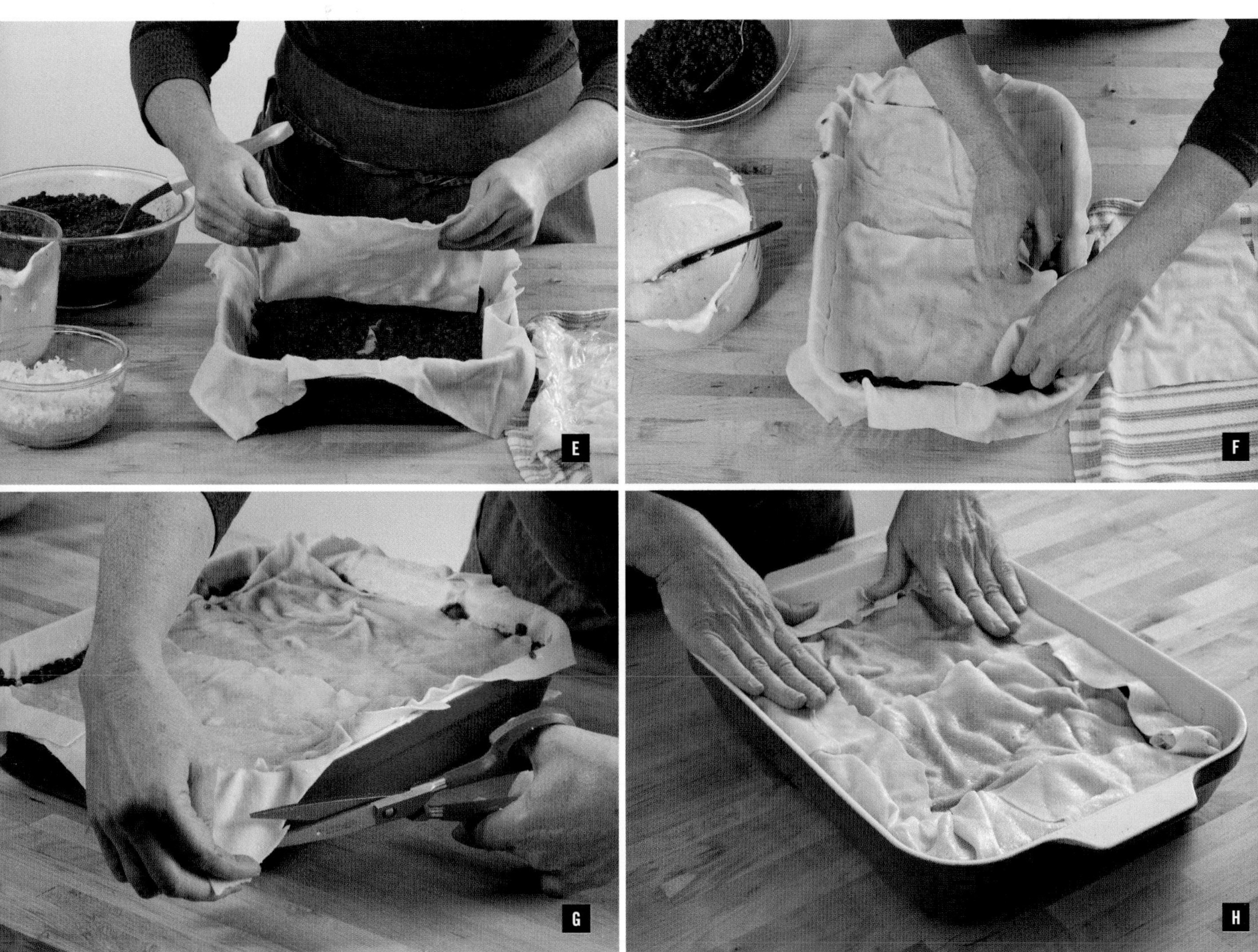
E F G H

14 Spread a thin layer of besciamella sauce over top and sprinkle with the remaining cheeses **(I)**.

15 Finished lasagna ready to bake **(J)**. (If desired, cover and refrigerate the lasagna up to 2 days before baking. Allow 1 hour, 15 minutes for baking if the lasagna is cold from the refrigerator.)

16 Bake 45 minutes, or until browned and bubbling on top and when a skewer stuck into the centre is hot to the touch **(K)**. Remove from the oven and allow the lasagna to cool for about 15 minutes so it sets up before cutting and serving.

I

J

K

CANNELLONI

A RICH CELEBRATION DISH, cannelloni started appearing in Italian culinary dictionaries only about one hundred fifty years ago. In the twentieth century, recipes for cannelloni stuffed with meat, topped with a creamy sauce, and gratinéed in the oven started to appear. Cannelloni means "big tube" and gets its name from *canna*, the cane plant, the same source for *cannella*, the Italian word for cinnamon, and for cannoli. Chicken thighs make for a moister filling with stronger "chickeny" flavour, though you may substitute milder chicken breasts, preferably on the bone for moistness, poaching them for about 15 minutes so they don't overcook.

1 quart (950 ml) rich chicken stock
1½ pounds (675 g) boneless, skinless chicken thighs or 3 pounds (1.4 kg) chicken thighs on the bone
½ pound (225 g) mature spinach (baby spinach is so tender that it will disappear)
5 tablespoons (75 g) unsalted butter
6 tablespoons (50 g) all-purpose flour
Fine sea salt, freshly ground black pepper, and freshly grated nutmeg to taste
1 cup (235 ml) heavy cream, scalded
Grated zest of 2 lemons (2 tablespoons, or 12 g)
Juice of 1 lemon (3 tablespoons, or 45 ml)
3 ounces (75 g), or about 1¼ cups, grated Parmigiano-Reggiano or Grana Padano cheese
2 tablespoons (8 g) finely chopped Italian parsley, for garnish
1 pound (450 g) firm Spinach Pasta Dough (page 53)
Extra flour for rolling

Yield: 16 to 24 cannelloni, serves 8 to 12

PREPARE THE FILLING:

1 Bring the stock to a boil in a large pot. Add the chicken thighs, bring the liquid back to a boil, then reduce heat to a simmer. Cook the chicken until tender, about 25 minutes. Cool and drain, reserving both broth and chicken. Pick off any connective tissue and fat pockets from the chicken, then chop the meat into small bits and reserve.

2 Wash the spinach in a large bowl of cold water, swishing around vigorously to encourage any sand to fall to the bottom of the bowl. Scoop the spinach from the water and transfer to a medium pot with a lid. Heat, covered, 2 to 3 minutes, stirring once or twice, cooking until the spinach has wilted completely. Drain the spinach and rinse under cold water to stop the cooking and set the colour. Drain again and then squeeze the spinach lightly to remove about half of its liquid. Chop the spinach into small bits and reserve.

PREPARE THE SAUCE:

3 In a medium heavy-bottomed pot, melt the butter and stir in the flour. Cook together over medium heat until light tan in colour, about 3 minutes. Whisk in the reserved chicken stock. Bring to a boil, whisking constantly so the sauce is smooth. Season generously to taste and remove from the heat. Cover sauce with a lid or directly with plastic wrap to prevent a skin from forming and cool.

4 Combine the reserved chicken, spinach, and 2 cups (475 ml) of the sauce for the filling. Stir the cream, lemon zest and juice, and half the cheese into the remaining sauce and reserve.

ROLL THE PASTA:

5 Roll out the pasta dough into sheets slightly thicker than for cut pasta strips because you will be cooking it twice. Cut into twenty-four 4-inch (10-cm) squares, preferably using a ridged cutter. Shown here **(A)** is a double-sided adjustable cutter (ideal).

6 Bring a large wide pot of salted water to a boil. Lay out several clean kitchen towels on a work surface to use for draining the pasta sheets. Add the pasta sheets to the water, cooking them in 2 or 3 batches. Boil until the pasta is about half-cooked and scoop from the water using a wire skimmer or slotted spoon. Transfer to a colander and drain, then run cold water over the pasta to rinse off the surface starch and stop the cooking. Drain again.

7 Arrange the cooked dough squares in a single layer on the towels **(B)**. Repeat until all the pasta squares are cooked. (Try to work quickly, as the pasta sheets will start to stick to the towels once they drain completely.)

8 Align the cooked pasta sheets in a grid before starting to fill them so you can use a more or less equal amount of filling for each square.

9 Preheat the oven to 375°F (190°C, or gas mark 5). To assemble the cannelloni, pour a thin layer of sauce into the bottom of a medium rectangular casserole **(C)**.

10 Divide the filling in half. Spread about ¼ cup (60 ml) of the filling across the centre of half of the pasta squares, leaving them open **(D)**. Repeat with the remaining squares and the remaining half of the filling. If you run out of filling, you can "steal" some from the other sheets.

11 Roll all the squares tightly, like a flute, leaving the ridged edge on top. Use your middle fingers to compact the filling and push it away from the edge **(E)**.

12 Arrange the cannelloni parallel to each other in the baking dish with their seams facing up **(F)**.

13 Push them in gently so they are tightly packed **(G)**.

14 Drizzle the remaining sauce over top, then sprinkle with the remaining cheese **(H)**.

15 Bake 40 minutes, or until browned and bubbling. Allow the cannelloni to cool about 10 minutes to set up, then sprinkle with parsley just before serving **(I)**.

E

F

G

H

I

CHAPTER **SIX**

MAKING CUT PASTA

THE ITALIAN *pastasciutta*, literally "dry pasta," refers to pasta in sauce as opposed to "wet" pasta in broth, and it is the ideal way to use the ribbons of pasta in this chapter. Broader strips such as pappardelle are usually dressed with rich, meaty ragù; thinner strips, such as fettuccine and tagliatelle, are dressed with light creamy sauces, fresh tomato sauce, or simply with butter or extra-virgin olive oil and grated cheese. The thinnest pasta strips such as tagliolini and cappellini are cooked and served in broth.

Tagliatelle, according to legend, was invented in 1501 when Zaffirino, court cook of Giovanni II Bentivoglio, served them to Lucrezia Borgia when he was inspired by her blonde tresses. Today, a regulation-size golden tagliatella (the singular form) that is 8 mm (about ¼ inch) wide may be found in the office of Bologna's Chamber of Commerce.

A FETTUCCINE BY ANY OTHER NAME

The names for various shapes and sizes of pasta in Italy change freely according to sauce and type of flour and region, and are often in dialect. Whole wheat fettuccine complete with bran becomes *lane pelose* (hairy wool) for its coarse texture, while fettuccine with goose ragù served for the harvest becomes *maccheroni* when dressed with honey and walnuts for Christmas Eve. Fettuccine get their name from the noun *fetta*, a slice, while the similar tagliatelle get their name from the verb *tagliare*, to cut.

Hand-cut tagliolini made from all-yolk dough showing an Italian dough knife

In this chapter, you'll learn to make Alsatian nouilles rolled out paper thin; hair-thin cappellini black with squid ink; pasta alla chitarra, Abruzzo's signature pasta cut into fat strings on a guitarlike contraption; spinach and egg "straw and hay" tagliatelle from Bologna; porcini tagliatelle rich with the earthy aromas of wild mushrooms; hearty buckwheat pizzoccheri from the Veneto; and thick, soft wheat flour udon noodles from Japan.

TIP: Slicing a sheet of rolled-up pasta dough to make individual noodles such as pappardelle, Alsatian nouilles, or fettuccine is easiest if using a sharp knife with a long straight blade such as an Italian dough knife (shown above), a Chinese or Japanese cleaver, or a santoku knife, rather than a curve-bladed chef's knife.

A WORLD OF **ASIAN NOODLES**

CHINESE NOODLES

WHEAT FLOUR NOODLES

LA MIAN

Literally "pulled noodles," these fresh noodles are made from wheat flour dough that is repeatedly stretched and folded to align the gluten proteins and warm up the dough in a technique that takes a great deal of skill and practice to master. The dough is then stretched out and folded again repeatedly to obtain thin noodles. A thicker spiced version called *laghman* is considered the national dish of Kyrgyzstan.

LO MEIN

Meaning "stirred and tossed noodles" in Cantonese, these chewy noodles made from wheat flour and egg or water are briefly cooked in boiling water, then briefly stir-fried with vegetables and meat or seafood and served with abundant bold sauces based on soy, oysters, and bean paste.

MEE POK

These wheat flour noodles are usually factory produced and may be made with egg. Lye gives them a deep yellow colour, springy texture, and distinctive aroma. These noodles require substantial preparation before cooking: separating, cutting, and blanching them in hot and cold water before tossing with a sauce made from chili, oil, vinegar, soy sauce, and pepper.

MISUA

These thin, fine noodles made from salted wheat flour dough cook in just 2 minutes. They are symbolic of long life in Chinese culture and are a traditional birthday food. Misua are usually topped with ingredients such as egg, oysters, shiitake mushrooms, beef, scallions, toasted nuts, and pork hocks or innards.

SAANG MEIN

These are quick-cooking noodles mainly sold in Hong Kong. They are made from soft wheat flour, tapioca flour, salt, and water. Potassium carbonate, an alkaline chemical compound also used in the production of soap, tenderises the dough and gives the noodles their smooth, slightly soapy texture. Saang mein is always served hot, seasoned with sesame oil and sometimes served with hard-cooked eggs and meat.

YOU MIAN (THIN NOODLES)

These Chinese noodles made with egg are widely used in Hong Kong and Guangdong as well as in Shanghai, Malaysia, and Singapore. They are usually boiled in broth with vegetables or stir-fried. They are often purchased precooked and are served hot or cold.

RICE AND BEAN STARCH NOODLES

FĔN SĪ (CELLOPHANE NOODLES OR BEAN THREADS)

Also known as Chinese vermicelli, crystal noodles, or glass noodles, fĕn sī are translucent starch-based noodles of irregular thickness and light gray or brownish-gray when cooked with soft, slippery, springy texture. Sold in dried bunches, these noodles are made from mung beans, yams, potatoes, and cassava (manioc) starch, and water. They are usually boiled and served in soups, stir-fries, braises, or used as spring roll filling. They can be deep-fried for a crunchy garnish.

LAI FUN

Long or short, these thick noodles are most commonly found in Hong Kong. They are made from ground sticky rice flour and tapioca starch and resemble Italian spaghetti and Asian silver needle noodles but have a straight cut rather than tapered end. Their Vietnamese equivalent is bánh canh.

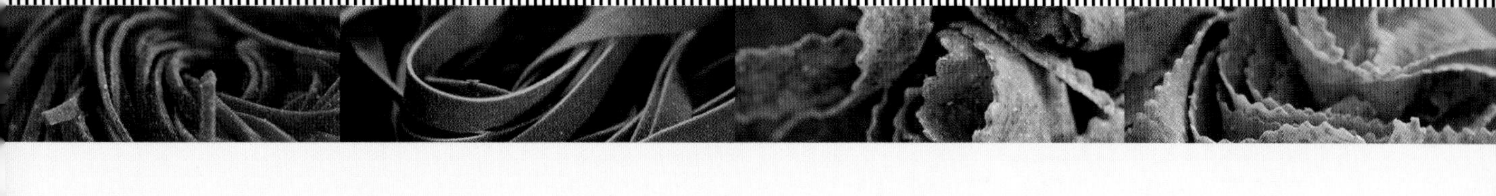

MI FEN (RICE VERMICELLI)
These thin semitranslucent rice flour–based noodles of uneven thickness are also known as rice noodles or rice sticks. They are sold in "bird's nests" and are a favourite in China, Hong Kong, Taiwan, Malaysia, and Vietnam. Mi fen may be deep-fried, expanding into puffy white sticks for garnish. Stir-fried mi fen with curry powder, bean sprouts, soy sauce, and chiles are known as Singapore noodles.

SHAHE FEN
Broad and slippery, these white rice flour noodles have an elastic, chewy texture. They are sold fresh in strips or sheets to be cut into desired widths, or dried. They are similar to Vietnamese bánh pho noodles. The noodles are stir-fried with pork, beef, or other meats, vegetables, and soy in a dish known as *chao fen* or chow fun in Chinese restaurants.

YIN ZHEN FEN OR LAO SHU FEN
These short, white semitranslucent noodles, known as "silver needle noodles" in Hong Kong and Taiwan and "rat noodles" in Malaysia and Singapore, have a long flat tapered shape with a pointy tip. They are produced commercially from rice flour with cornstarch added to reduce breakage. The noodles may be stir-fried, soaked in boiling water, and flavoured with various sauces or cooked in soup.

JAPANESE NOODLES

RAMEN
These thin noodles are made from wheat flour, salt, water, and eggs or kansui, a mineral water, that imparts a yellowish colour and firm texture to the dough. The dough rises before being pulled into noodles. Ramen were imported from China to Japan during the Meiji period in the mid-nineteenth century, and are used in soup. They are the basis of instant ramen, which are precooked by deep-frying. Invented on August 25, 1958, it is commemorated as the "day of noodles" in Japan.

SHIRATAKI
Known as the "white waterfall," these clear Japanese noodles are made from the root of the Devil's Tongue (*Amorphophallus konjac*). They are chewy or rubbery, high in fibre, and low in carbohydrates and calories. Some manufacturers add tofu to the dough for tenderness. Shirataki noodles come packed in liquid and ready to eat after draining, adding texture to sukiyaki and oden, winter stews.

SOBA
These thin noodles are usually made from a combination of buckwheat and wheat flour. Chilled soba are accompanied by soba tsuyu, dipping sauce made from dashi, sweetened soy sauce, and mirin. They are often served chilled with dipping sauces in hot weather and in soups or other hot dishes in cold weather and are most popular in eastern Japan, near Tokyo.

SŌMEN
These are very thin, white, stretched noodles made from wheat flour often served as a cooling summer dish ice-chilled with dipping sauces similar to those served with soba and flavoured with scallions, ginger, or myoga, native Japanese ginger.

HAND-ROLLED ALSATIAN NOUILLES

THE GERMAN-INFLUENCED region of Alsace in France is the home of tender, rich French egg noodles. These nouilles are made with a little vinegar to help keep the dough tender. The dough is hand-rolled until thin enough to read the newspaper through (or at least the headlines), then cut into short, thin strips. Some of the noodles are toasted for crunch and colour, then mixed with noodles that have been boiled briefly and tossed with butter, chives, and poppy seeds.

6 ounces (170 g) unbleached all-purpose flour, plus extra flour for rolling
1 large egg, at room temperature
3 egg yolks
1 tablespoon (15 ml) tepid water
1 teaspoon vinegar
Pinch sea salt
1 tablespoon (15 ml) vegetable oil
3 tablespoons (45 g) unsalted butter
1 tablespoon (8 g) poppy seeds
1 tablespoon (3 g) thinly sliced chives
Fine sea salt and freshly ground black pepper to taste

Yield: 10 ounces (275 g), serves 3 to 4, serves 6 to 8 if served in soup

1 Place the flour and salt in a large mixing bowl making a "volcano." In a small bowl, whisk together the egg, yolks, water, vinegar, and salt. Pour into the "crater" in the centre, then use a fork to start incorporating the flour. Continue following the technique in Basic Egg Pasta Dough (page 31). Knead until the dough is cohesive and moderately smooth. Wrap in plastic film and allow the dough to rest at room temperature for 1 hour.

2 Divide the dough into 2 and press each piece into a rough rectangle. Cover the second piece with a damp towel or enclose in plastic wrap to prevent a skin from forming. Follow the directions in Hand-Stretched Pasta Dough (page 42) to roll out until the sheet is thin enough to see the grain of wood of the worktable.

3 The classic thickness test is to place a newspaper underneath the sheet of dough. If you can read the newspaper, the dough is thin enough **(A)**. Otherwise, keep rolling and stretching.

4 Using a very sharp knife so as not to mash the dough strips, cut the sheet of dough into 2-inch (5-cm)–wide strips, using a ruler to mark off the lengths **(B)**.

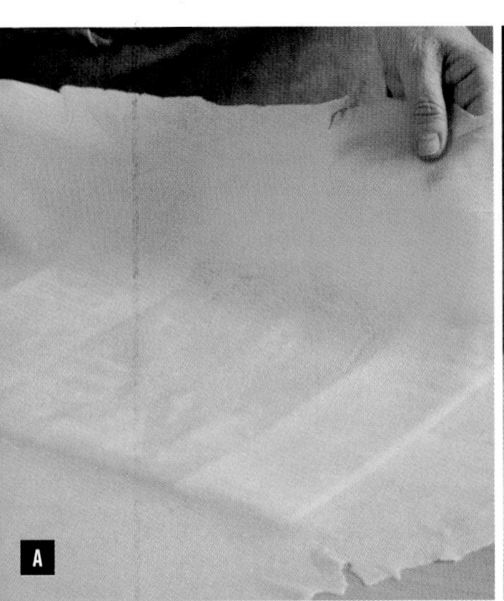
A

B

C

5 Stack the dough strips, dusting lightly with flour in between (C). Next, divide the stack of strips into piles of 2 or 3 strips.

6 Using a very sharp knife so as not to mash the noodles, cut the dough strips crosswise into ¼-inch (6-mm)–wide strips (D).

7 Lift the pasta strips and toss to separate the cut strips into individual noodles (E). If the dough is tacky, dust lightly with flour so the noodles will not be gluey when you cook them.

Place the cut noodles on a mesh drying rack to dry for about 30 minutes, keeping them separated.

COOK THE NOODLES:

8 Heat the vegetable oil in a medium skillet and add 1 cup (235 ml) of the uncooked noodles. Brown well over moderate heat, shaking the pan often so the noodles brown evenly. Drain excess oil and reserve.

9 Bring a large pot of salted water to a boil. Add the remaining noodles and cook until tender but still yellow in colour and chewy in texture, about 3 minutes. Drain well.

10 Meanwhile, heat the butter in a large skillet until it turns golden brown. Add the poppy seeds, chives, salt, and pepper, and toss to combine. Add the drained, cooked noodles and toss again. Serve immediately, garnished with fried noodles (F).

PASTA IN FRANCE

Jewish immigrants from Italy brought their knowledge of making pasta to France in the eleventh century. The people of Alsace got their taste for egg noodles from Italian soldiers billeted there during the Thirty Years War (1618–1648).

D

E

F

CAPPELLINI

HERE BLACK SQUID INK pasta is cut into cappellini, fine as hair (*capelli* in Italian). Cappellini are perfect for soaking up delicious broth made from shrimp, calamari, scallops, fish, clams, mussels, or other "fruits of the sea."

1 pound (450 g) Squid Ink Pasta Dough (page 59)
Extra flour for rolling

Yield: 1 pound (450 g), serves 4 to 6

IDEAS FOR SEAFOOD BROTHS

- Steamed clams with garlic, olive oil, hot pepper flakes, and white wine
- Calamari rings with fresh diced tomato, capers, oregano, and chopped green olives
- Shrimp with olive oil, hot pepper flakes, garlic, thin strips of zucchini skin, thyme, and dry white vermouth

1 Divide the squid ink dough into 4 portions, keeping all but 1 covered so they stay moist. Flour the pasta sheet generously as you handle it as this dough is rather sticky. Roll out the dough into sheets following the directions for Rolling Pasta Dough with a Sheeter (page 45) **(A)**. Arrange the sheets on a mesh pasta drying tray or a collapsible pasta drying rack. Allow the dough sheets to dry for at least 30 minutes at room temperature, flipping them over once. The sheets will be ready to cut when the surface on both sides is dry and has the texture of smooth cardboard.

2 Attach the cappellini cutter to the front of the pasta machine. Run the sheets through the cutter, supporting the cut pasta with your hands to keep the strands separated **(B)**.

3 Dust the cut squid ink pasta generously with semolina to keep the strands separate. Roll a handful of pasta into individual nests, twisting the strands while rolling **(C)**.

4 Handle the nests carefully as this pasta is fragile **(D)**. To cook, boil briefly in salted water then serve with thin seafood-based broth.

A

B

C

D

PORCINI TAGLIATELLE

HERE, FRAGRANT WOODSY brown porcini pasta is cut into tagliatelle using the cutter attachment for the pasta machine. Cook and serve *alla boscaiola*, woodsmen's style (with mushroom, herb, and tomato sauce) or with a light cream sauce infused with reconstituted dried porcini mushrooms along with their tasty mushroom liquor - or soaking juices. Marsala wine (not the sweet "dolce" kind), brandy, rosemary, thyme, sage, red onion, garlic, and cured meats such as pancetta and prosciutto all complement this type of pasta.

1¼ pounds (565 g) Porcini Mushroom Pasta Dough (page 57)
Extra flour for rolling

Yield: 1¼ pounds (465 g), serves 6 to 8

1. Divide the dough into 4 sections, keeping all but 1 covered with plastic wrap to keep them moist.

2. Roll out 1 section of porcini pasta following the directions for Rolling Pasta Dough with a Sheeter on page 45 **(A)**. Allow the sheets to dry until their surface is dry but the pasta is not brittle, about 20 minutes.

3. Attach the cutter to the front of the pasta machine by inserting the sides into the lengthwise slots on the side and cut into the tagliatelle. Dust the sheet lightly with flour and feed it through the cutter, supporting the sheet over your hand and wrist to feed the sheet straight through the machine without twisting. Crank slowly while maintaining pressure **(B)**.

4. Allow the cut strips to air-dry until their surface is no longer moist. Take a half-handful of tagliatelle strips and roll them up together to make individual nests, twisting once **(C)**.

5. Place the porcini nests on a mesh pasta drying rack. Either cook right away or allow the nests to dry completely before cooking **(D)**. Each nest is usually a half or whole portion.

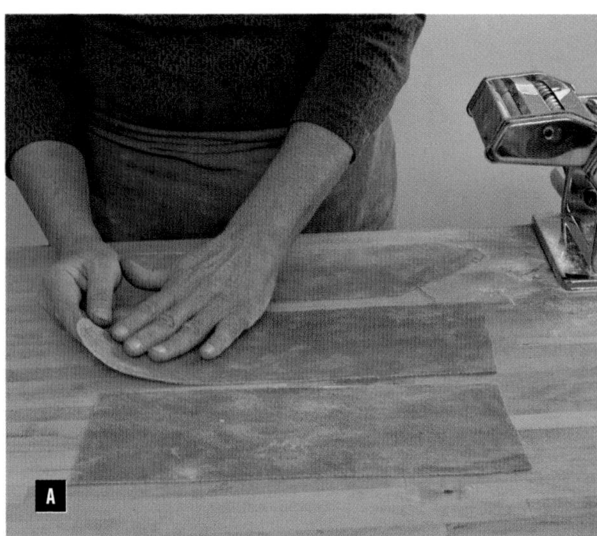
A

B

C

D

STRAW AND HAY

THESE ARE NESTS rolled from two coloured pastas - egg and spinach fettuccine - with the fanciful Italian name, *paglia e fieno*, straw and hay, that is reminiscent of golden straw and green hay. This is a relatively modern pasta that does not appear in the Renato Rovetta's manual, *Industria del pastificio o dei maccheroni* (pasta and macaroni maker's industry) published in 1951, a listing of factory-made pasta shapes found in Italy. Straw and hay is often served in a cream sauce with sautéed strips of prosciutto, young green peas, and Parmigiano cheese.

½ pound (225 g) Basic Egg Pasta Dough (page 30)
½ pound (225 g) Spinach Pasta Dough (page 53)
Extra flour for rolling

Yield: 1 pound (450 g), serves 4 to 6

1 Roll out each type of pasta following the directions for Rolling Pasta Dough with a Sheeter (page 45). Allow the sheets to dry until their surface is dry but the pasta is not brittle, about 20 minutes **(A)**.

2 Use a rolling multiple-bladed cutter to cut the pasta into strips **(B)**.

3 Pull away individual strips that are still semiattached to each other to separate them **(C)**.

4 Grasp a half-handful of each type of pasta **(D)** and roll them up together to make individual nests.

Or, roll out egg pasta and spinach pasta sheets and cut each using the fettuccine attachment on the machine. Combine half egg and half spinach strips to make each nest.

5 Either cook right away, allow the nests to dry completely, or cover and refrigerate up to 3 days before cooking. Each nest is usually a half or whole portion **(E)**.

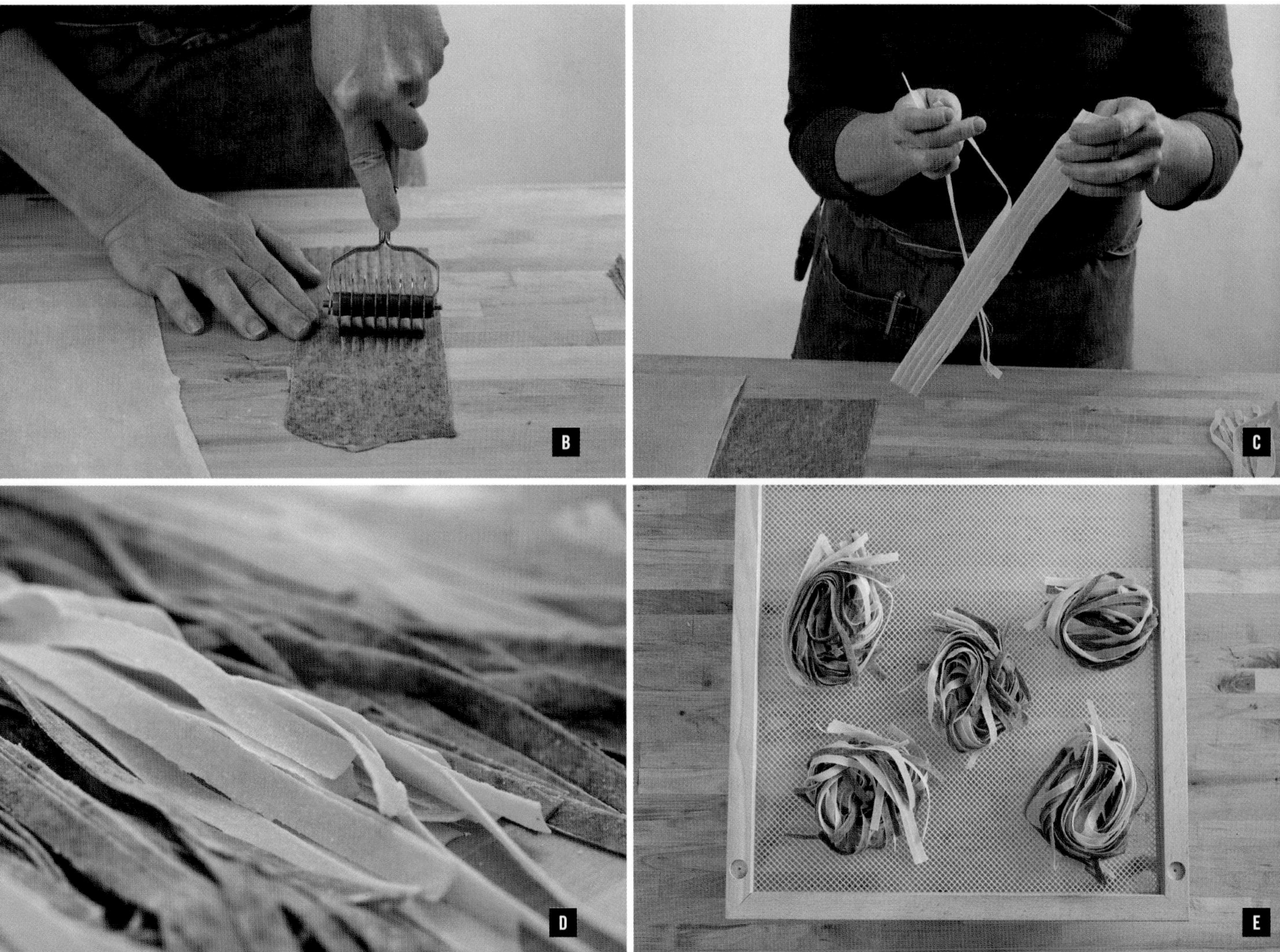

A

B

C

D

PAPPARDELLE AND TAGLIOLINI

PAPPARDELLE ARE wide egg pasta ribbons usually served with a hearty ragù of feathered game, such as pigeon and duck, or furred game, such as hare and wild boar in Tuscany, where they are most commonly found. Pappardelle have been made for at least 400 years and get their name from the Tuscan dialect verb *pappare*, meaning "to gobble." Tagliolini are narrow noodles best suited to cooking and serving in soup and often made from all-yolk dough for richness and supple texture, and because the protein bonds formed by the dough make it strong enough not to shatter when cut thinly.

1¼ pounds (565 g) Basic Egg Pasta Dough (page 30) or ¾ pound (350 g) Hand-Stretched Pasta Dough (page 42)
Extra flour for rolling

Yield: 1¼ pounds (565 g) if using the Basic Egg Pasta Dough, serves 6 to 8; ¾ pound (350 g) if using Hand-Stretched Pasta Dough, serves 3 to 4

1 Place the sheet of dough, here hand-stretched, onto a clean cotton cloth and cover with a second cloth **(A)**. Allow the dough sheet to dry for about 15 minutes or until the surface is dry but not brittle, turning once or twice (especially in humid weather). Dust lightly with more flour (especially in humid weather).

2 If using Basic Egg Pasta Dough, roll into sheets following the directions on page 43. Cut each length into individual sheets about 12 inches (30 cm) long. Arrange on a mesh pasta drying rack or a hanging pasta rack and allow the sheets to dry until their surface is dry but not at all brittle, turning once or twice (especially in humid weather).

3 To cut wider pappardelle (here made with egg dough) or thinner tagliolini (here made with all-yolk dough), roll up the sheet of dough from both ends toward the middle to make a double tube **(B & C)**. Fold one tube over top of the other to make a compact tube.

4 Begin to cut slices from the dough of even width, 8 to 10 mm (⅓ to ½ inch) for fettuccine and 1.5 to 2.5 cm (6⁄10 to 1 inch) for pappardelle **(D)** using a sharp dough knife (as shown), Japanese santoku knife, or chef's knife. Keep the knife at a 90-degree angle to the dough tube.

5 For tagliolini, use all egg-yolk dough and cut into very thin strips, as thin and even as possible. Keep the knife at a 90-degree angle to the roll of pasta so you don't end up with zigzag strips **(E)**.

If desired, save the trimmings to cut into maltagliati (page 82), keeping them moist in a plastic bag.

6 Run your fingers down the centre of a portion of dough strips and lift up, allowing the dough strips to unravel in both directions **(F)**.

7 Shake the strips to separate them **(G)**. Dust lightly with flour.

8 Gently roll up, adding a twist, and form into a nest **(H)**. Each nest may be 1 portion or 2 nests may equal a portion, but keep the weight of the nests even, using a scale if desired. A main course portion will weigh about ¼ pound (115 g).

Arrange on a mesh pasta drying rack for drying. Or, arrange on a semolina-dusted tray, cover lightly with plastic wrap and keep refrigerated up to 3 days before cooking.

NOTE: The wider the pasta, the more brittle it will be when dried, so handle pappardelle with care. The easiest way to work with pappardelle is to roll them out and cook them the same day with a minimum of drying involved.

E

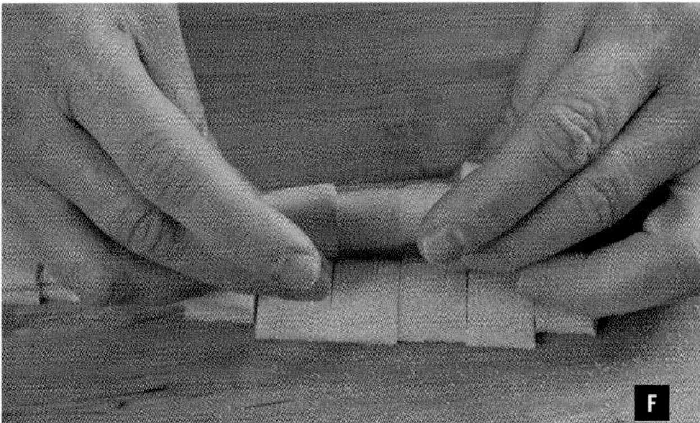
F

G

H

PASTA ALLA CHITARRA

THE WIRE-STRINGED metal or wood-framed instrument known as a *chitarra*, Italian for guitar, is a symbol of the mountainous Italian region of Abruzzo. The chitarra originated around 1800 in the province of Chieti. The pasta cut with it is a form of square-sided spaghetti, about 12 inches (30 cm) long. It is known as tonnarelli in the adjoining province of Lazio, where Rome is located. In Abruzzo, pasta alla chitarra is traditionally tossed with mutton (mature lamb) ragù. (See the recipe for Lamb Ragù on page 119.)

18 ounces (500 g) Whole Wheat Pasta Dough (page 37) or 1 pound (450 g) Semolina Pasta Dough (page 39)
Extra flour for rolling

Yield: 18 ounces (500 g) if using Whole Wheat Pasta Dough, serves 5 to 6; 1 pound (450 g) if using Semolina Pasta Dough, serves 4 to 6

1. Divide the dough into 4 sections and roll out 1 at a time to medium thickness (about number 4 on an Atlas machine). Cut into lengths about 1 inch (2.5 cm) shorter on either end as the length of the "guitar strings," because rolling out will lengthen the strands. Allow the sheets to dry at room temperature for about 15 minutes or until the surface is dry and feels like smooth cardboard.

2. Lay a sheet of the pasta (whole wheat used here) over the strings. Using a rolling pin, apply gentle pressure while rolling the pin over the pasta up and down the wires several times **(A)**.

   You should be able to see the wire strings appear through the dough **(B & C)**.

   To detach the strings, run your fingertips up and down the wires **(D)** until the pasta strings start to drop through onto the collection board below **(E & F)**.

3. Dust the cut pasta strings lightly with flour so they don't stick together, then allow them to dry at room temperature until their surface is dry to the touch. Hang on a rod-type pasta drying rack or roll up into a pasta "nest" and allow the pasta to dry completely or cook as desired.

NOTE: If the pasta sheet elongates too much when rolling so that either end is beyond the end of the wires, snip off a strip from each end with kitchen shears.

A
B
C
D
E
F

BUCKWHEAT PIZZOCCHERI

PIZZOCCHERI ARE made from buckwheat flour, wheat flour, and a liquid, which may be water, milk and/or eggs. Buckwheat pasta is brittle because it contains no gluten, so the dough is rolled out thicker than other doughs. Pizzoccheri get their name from two words: pita, "bread" in Arabic, and *bizzochi*, a sect of monks who wore gray, the same dark colour as the pasta. Arabs brought buckwheat to Italy, where it is known as *grana saraceno*, or "Saracen grain." The hearty dark noodles are typically cooked with potatoes and savoy cabbage and sauced with melted butter and rich, melting mountain cheese, especially Casera and Bitto, though Italian Fontina works well too.

1¼ pounds (565 g), Buckwheat Pasta Dough (page 38)
Extra flour for rolling

Yield: 1¼ pounds (565 g), serves 6 to 8

1 Divide the dough into 4 sections. Roll out 1 section at a time using the pasta sheeter (see page 45), rolling moderately thick, about number 5 on an Atlas machine.

A

2 Place the sheet of buckwheat pasta on a wooden work surface and cut into 1½- or 2½-inch (4- or 6-cm)–wide strips, using a ridged cutter if desired **(A)**. (Here we use a double adjustable ridged cutter.)

3 Remove the edge strips, saving them if desired for rerolling **(B)**. (If so, wrap in plastic and allow the scraps to rest for at least 1 hour before rerolling to relax the gluten.)

4 Next, cut the strips on the short side into short strips about ¾ to 1¼ inch (2 to 3 cm) wide **(C)**. Cutting on an angle will create rhomboid-shaped noodles.

5 Dust the cut pizzoccheri lightly with flour so they don't stick together. Cook immediately or allow them to dry at room temperature until their surface is dry to the touch before storing, or cover and refrigerate up to 3 days before cooking.

Shown here is an old ridged pasta cutting wheel made from bronze, which takes a sharp edge so it is ideal for cutting pasta. Most cutting wheels are now made from stainless steel or aluminum.

B

C

JAPANESE UDON NOODLES

UDON NOODLES are thick, smooth, chewy wheat flour noodles usually served in noodle soup. Korean low-protein (9 percent) flour yields tender noodles; Italian 00 or pastry flour are also good choices. The dough is made with warm water to encourage gluten formation. Serve udon noodles in a bowl with soupy sauce meant for dipping made from dashi (kombu kelp and shavings of katsuobushi - preserved, fermented tuna), soy sauce, and mirin (thick, sweet rice wine), topped with thinly sliced scallions and garnishes such as grated ginger and strips of shiso leaves on the side.

½ teaspoon fine sea salt
¼ cup plus 1 tablespoon (75 ml) warm water
10 ounces (275 g) flour, preferably Korean low-protein flour, Italian 00, or pastry flour, plus extra flour for rolling

Yield: about 1 pound (450 g), serves 4 to 6

1. Dissolve the salt in the warm water, stirring until it is completely dissolved. Place the flour in a large mixing bowl. Pour the salted water over the flour a little at a time while tossing it with the flour until you have added all the water and it is evenly distributed.

2. Continue to mix the dough until it forms a cohesive mass, then transfer to a work surface and knead the dough until it is shiny and elastic, about 10 minutes. The dough should be soft and silky. Use a rolling pin to press it out into a thin round, then wrap it in plastic wrap and set aside to rest at room temperature for 1 to 2 hours to relax the gluten.

3. Sprinkle flour over a cutting board, preferably wood. Divide the dough in half, cover the second piece with a damp towel, or enclose in plastic wrap to prevent a skin from forming on the surface. Place one-half at a time on the board and roll it into a large rectanglelike shape between ⅛ inch (3 mm) and ¼ inch (6 mm) thick, about twice the thickness of Italian tagliatelle **(A)**.

4. Sprinkle more flour over the dough, then roll it into a long tube **(B)**.

5. Using a very sharp knife so as not to mash the dough strips, cut the sheet of dough crosswise into strips about ⅕ inch (5 mm) wide **(C & D)**. (Cutting against a steel ruler makes this step easier.)

6. Unroll the noodles **(E)**.

7. Toss the noodles generously with more flour to prevent them from sticking together **(F)**. A main course portion will weigh about ¼ pound (115 g).

8. Cook fresh udon noodles **(G)** as soon as possible after making them as they get brittle if dried.

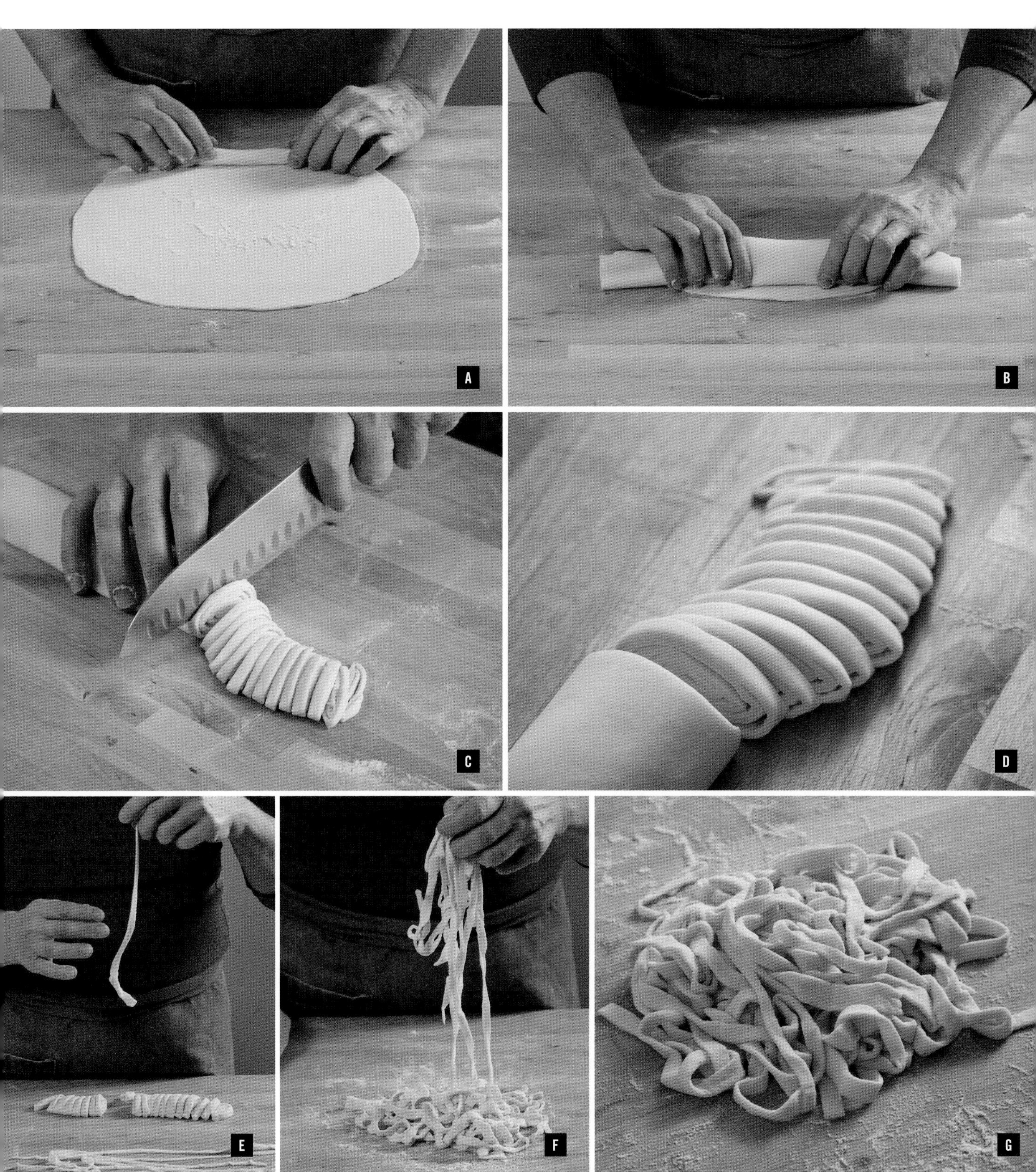
A
B
C
D
E
F
G

CHAPTER SEVEN

SPECIALTY HAND-FORMED PASTA

IN THIS CHAPTER, you will find many unusual hand-shaped and cut pasta shapes including cavatelli from Puglia, the similar malloreddus from Sardinia, decorative coin-shaped corzetti from Genoa, and the small hand-rolled pasta tubes known as garganelli from Emilia-Romagna.

Most of the pastas in this chapter are made from special doughs whose recipes are included with the techniques. Also in this chapter are Umbrian ombrichelli, which are made from the simplest soft wheat flour and water and hand-formed into spaghetti-like strands. Greek trahana are small coarse pieces of dough made from flour and yogurt or vegetable purée that are dried and then crumbled.

These are some of the simplest and oldest forms of pasta mostly formed by hand. However, to make them quickly and uniformly requires hand-skill, good instruction, and a bit of practice.

TRADITIONAL PASTA SAUCES

These traditional pastas and their accompanying sauces developed over many years guided by local, seasonal products and, in Italy especially, the church calendar. During Lent, when meat and often dairy products are not eaten, pasta is dressed with olive oil, vegetables, and legumes, often paired with greens for flavour and better digestibility.

Until World War II, the great majority of Italians living outside the cities ate pasta only on feast days, usually in soup with legumes (*pasta e fagioli*). Meat was scarce, so meat sauces were reserved for special occasions and often involved tasty but difficult-to-cook innards. When a large cut of meat or a whole bird was cooked for pasta sauce or broth, the meat would be served as a separate course.

The tomato, which arrived in Southern Italy in the mid-sixteenth century from the Spanish, flourished in the region around Naples where today small pointy-ended Piennolo (hanging) tomatoes grown in mineral-rich volcanic soil on the slopes of Mount Vesuvius are still prized. Tomato sauce didn't become popular in Italian kitchens until the end of the nineteenth century. In Liguria, men went to sea for months at a time surviving on salt meat and hardtack biscuits. Upon their return, they craved fresh greens,

NOTE: When making pasta "snakes" as for the cavatelli, orecchiette, and ombrichelli in this chapter, extend your hand past the edge of the pasta when you roll to keep the ends from being fatter than the centre.

Ricotta cavatelli (left) and barley-saffron malloreddus (right)

so Genoese pasta is often made with fresh herbs or greens such as nettles, borage, and marjoram in the dough or is dressed with herb sauces such as basil pesto. In the wealthier north, especially in Emilia-Romagna, local cheese, butter, cream, and cured meats were and still are used with abandon for pasta sauces and stuffing. In Piemonte, with its strong French influence, pasta sauces made from the rich juices of braised meats also include precious local truffles. In the Veneto, onion sauce with sardines or anchovies for whole wheat bigoli (thick homemade spaghetti) is so common that is it simply known as "salsa."

PASTA SHAPES AND BODY PARTS

Pasta shapes are often reminiscent of parts of the body, including the three ear-shaped pastas in this book: Chinese Cat's Ear Noodles (Mao Er Duo), Pugliese Orecchiette, and Siberian Pelmeni (Chapter Eight).

RICOTTA CAVATELLI FROM PUGLIA

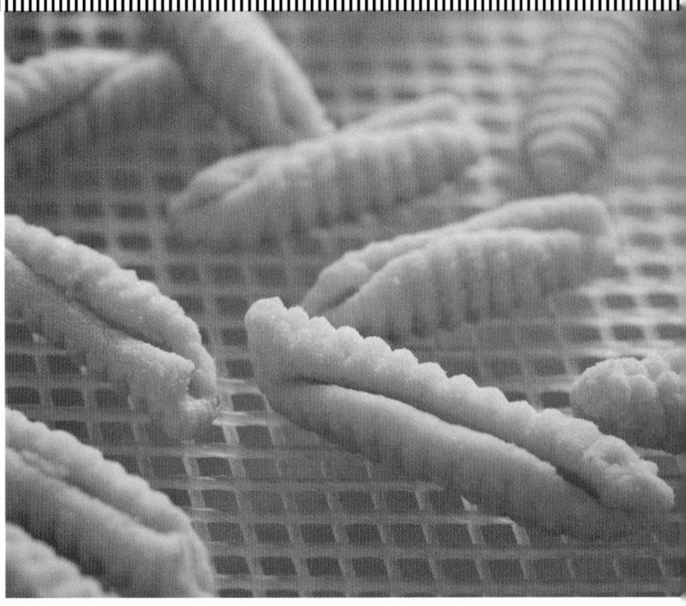

CAVATELLI (cavatieddi in Pugliese dialect) get their name from the word "cavato," which means indented - like "cave" in English. These bite-size ridged, curled-up pasta rolls are often made with durum flour from Puglia and firm ricotta cheese.
(To make them in the old style, after forming it into finger-thick "snakes," the dough is cut into small coins. Using a special iron tool called a sferre, the coins are drawn across a carved wooden board, curling the pieces of dough while embossing a pattern on the outside.) Here, we feed the snake through a mechanical cavatelli maker - much easier. Cavatelli are boiled with *cime di rapa* (turnip greens), broccoli rabe, or wild rucola (arugula), and seasoned with grated sharp cacio cheese.

1 pound (450 g) durum flour
1 container (15 ounces, or 425 g) or 1 pound (450 g) thick whole milk ricotta cheese, drained if at all soupy
2 large eggs, at room temperature

Yield: 34 ounces (1 kg) cavatelli, serves 8 to 12

1 Pour the flour into a large bowl or onto a wooden work surface or board and form the "volcano," with a well in the centre. Place the eggs and ricotta cheese into the "crater." Using a fork and working in a circular fashion (clockwise if you're right-handed, counterclockwise if you're left-handed), begin incorporating the flour. Follow the directions for Basic Egg Pasta Dough on page 31 to complete the dough.

2 Divide the dough into 4 sections and cover 3 sections to keep them from drying out. Divide the remaining quarter into quarters again, covering 3 quarters (you'll eventually be making 12 "ropes"). Sprinkle the work

A

B

surface, preferably wooden, with flour and roll the dough into a long rope about the thickness of your index finger **(A)**.

3 Clamp a mechanical cavatelli machine to the edge of the table **(B)**.

Dust 1 rope generously with flour. Start feeding it between the 2 wooden cylinders while cranking the handle slowly, with an even speed **(C)**.

The dough will be cut and shaped and then come out the other side of the machine, dropping from one of the two small rotating metal baskets **(D & E)**.

4 As the cavatelli drop off the edge, pick them up and arrange them, touching each other as little as possible, on a mesh pasta drying rack or a clean cotton cloth that has been dusted with semolina or cornmeal. To streamline this process and to have more control over the size and shape of the cavatelli, one person can feed the rope into the machine and another can catch them at the other end.

5 Serve right away, cover and refrigerate up to 3 days, freeze (see page 40), or dry completely and store.

NOTE: If the cavatelli stick together at the side of the cavatelli machine opening rather than dropping down one at a time, the rope is too thick and/or the dough is too soft. Reroll the dough "snake" thinner and/or incorporate more flour. Allow the dough to rest again for at least 30 minutes after adding more flour so the gluten relaxes.

C

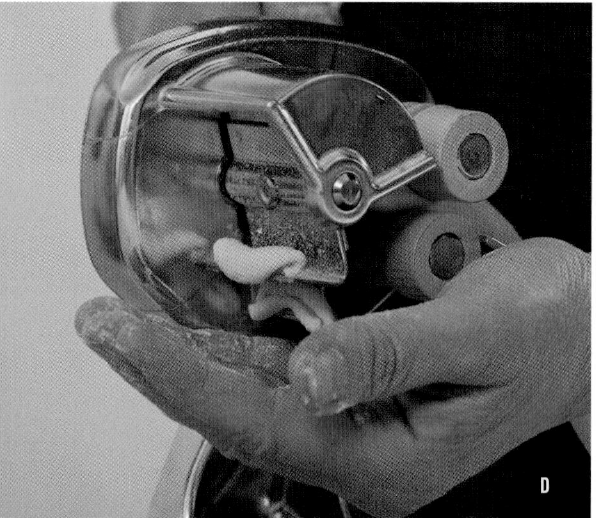
D

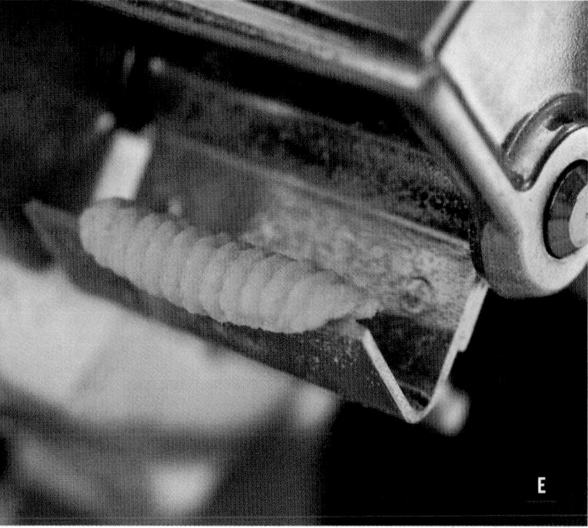
E

SARDINIAN MALLOREDDUS

MALLOREDDUS ARE MADE from the durum wheat that has grown in Sardinia since Roman times. Its name is a diminutive of the Latin *malleolus* (like malleable) for a type of gnoccho. Local saffron imparts a rich golden colour and recalls foods once decorated with gold leaf. Formerly, malloreddus were made from barley flour (used here), and were known as *maccarronis de orgiu* (barley) to be served with grated dried sheep's milk ricotta. The traditional method of making malloreddus was to cut ropes of dough into pieces, which were flattened with the pad of the thumb against the bottom of a wicker basket called a *ciurili*, forming bite-size ridged shell-shaped pasta. Malloreddus are usually served with hearty meat or sausage sauces seasoned with pecorino Sardo, or with fresh tomato and basil sauce.

1 large pinch saffron threads
¼ cup (60 ml) tepid water
½ pound (225 g) durum flour
¼ pound (115 g) barley flour (see how to grind your own flour on page 27)
3 large eggs, at room temperature

Yield: 1¼ pounds (565 g), serves 6 to 8

1. In a small bowl, soak the saffron in the water until the water turns orange-red, about 30 minutes, or up to overnight.
2. Combine the durum and barley flours (or substitute all durum) in a large mixing bowl. Pour the eggs and saffron mixture into the centre. Use a fork to work in the flour, following the instructions on page 31 for Basic Egg Pasta Dough.
3. Follow the instructions for Cavatelli (on page 116) to form the malloreddus.
4. Arrange the malloreddus on a mesh pasta drying rack so they do not touch each other. Allow them to dry completely before storing them up to 3 months.

A TRIO OF TRADITIONAL PASTA SAUCES

ROSE SAUCE

3 pounds (1.4 kg) red ripe plum tomatoes, peeled and seeded
¼ white onion, peeled
4 tablespoons (55 g) unsalted butter
Fine sea salt and freshly ground black pepper to taste
2 cups (475 ml) heavy cream
¼ cup (60 ml) thinly sliced strips of fresh basil
2 ounces (55 g), or about ¾ cup, grated Parmigiano-Reggiano cheese or Grana Padano

Dice 1 pound (450 g) of the tomatoes and reserve. Coarsely purée the remaining 2 pounds (900 g) tomatoes. In a nonreactive pot (not aluminum), simmer together the tomato purée, white onion, and butter, stirring occasionally for about 20 minutes or until thickened. Remove and discard the onion, season with salt and pepper, and reserve. Meanwhile, simmer the cream until reduced by half to 1 cup (235 ml) liquid.

Transfer the tomato purée, diced tomatoes, reduced cream, and basil strips to a wide shallow skillet and bring to a boil. Toss gently with pasta, such as Tortelloni (page 141) and cheese, and serve immediately.

Yield: serves 8 or more

BROWN BUTTER AND SAGE SAUCE

4 tablespoons (55 g) unsalted butter
2 tablespoons (5 g) whole sage leaves
2 ounces (55 g), or about ¾ cup, grated Parmigiano-Reggiano cheese or Grana Padano

In a large heavy-bottomed skillet, heat the butter over moderate heat until it turns nutty brown with an aroma of hazelnuts. Add the sage leaves and allow them to sizzle in the butter for 1 minute, or until fragrant. Remove the skillet from the heat. Toss the sauce gently with pasta, such as Caramelle (page 146) or Giant Asparagus Raviolo with Soft-Cooked Egg (page 158) until well-coated, then toss again with the grated cheese. Serve immediately, preferably on heated plates.

Yield: serves 6 to 8

LAMB RAGÙ

1½ pounds (675 g) boneless lamb shoulder
1 small red onion, peeled, trimmed, and cut into rough chunks
1 rib celery, washed and trimmed, cut into thick slices
1 carrot, peeled and trimmed, cut into thick slices
2 cloves garlic
Fine sea salt and freshly ground black pepper to taste
¼ cup (60 ml) extra-virgin olive oil
2 teaspoons each finely chopped fresh thyme and rosemary
1 cup (235 ml) dry red wine
1 container (26 ounces, or 750 ml) chopped plum tomatoes, preferably Pomì

Place the lamb in the freezer for 30 minutes or until firm but not hard. Trim off excess fat and cut into very small cubes. Reserve.

Preheat the oven to 300°F (150°C, or gas mark 2). Make a soffritto by placing the onion, celery, carrots, and garlic in the bowl of a food processor and process to small chunks or chop together finely by hand. Reserve.

Season the lamb with salt and pepper. Heat 2 tablespoons (30 ml) of the oil in a large heavy skillet and brown the lamb cubes well on all sides, working in several batches to maintain high temperature in the pan. Reserve the skillet. Transfer the lamb to a Dutch oven.

Add the remaining 2 tablespoons (30 ml) olive oil, herbs, and soffritto to the reserved skillet. Cook over medium heat until the vegetables are softened and most of the liquid has cooked away. Add to the lamb, wine, and tomatoes, mix well, cover, and bake 1 hour in the oven, or until oil rises to the top of the sauce and the meat is tender. Toss with pasta such as Pasta alla Chitarra (page 108).

Yield: serves 6 to 8

Franco Casoni, a wood carver and sculptor in Chiavari, south of Genoa on the Ligurian coast, is one of the few remaining carvers of the molds used to make corzetti, decorative Ligurian pasta coins.

GENOESE CHESTNUT CORZETTI

CORZETTI (croxetti or corsetti), which likely means "little crosses," were documented as early as the thirteenth century, and early designs are thought to have featured a Genoese crusader cross. During the Renaissance, prominent Ligurian families would have their coat of arms carved on one side of the stamp with symbols such as a sheaf of wheat or a flower blossom on the reverse. Neutral hard woods such as beech (*faggio* in Italian), maple, apple, and pear are best for the molds. Because the thin discs dried well, they were a good food for Genoa's sailors, who were off at sea for months.

10.5 ounces (300 g) Pasta Flour Mix (page 24), plus extra flour for rolling
3.5 ounces (100 g) chestnut flour (see Resources, page 168)
Pinch fine sea salt
¾ cup (175 ml) dry white wine
4 egg yolks

Yield: 18 ounces (500 g), serves 5 to 6

1 Whisk together the flour, chestnut flour, and salt in a large mixing bowl, forming a "volcano" in the centre with a "crater" in the middle. In a small bowl or measuring cup, combine the white wine and egg yolks and pour the mixture into the crater. Follow the instructions from Basic Egg Pasta Dough (page 31) to make the dough. Roll the dough into thick sheets, usually number 4 on a pasta sheeter.

2. Place a sheet of pasta dough on a wooden work surface, dusting on the top and bottom with flour, and cut out circles using the circular cutter on the underside of the corzetti stamp. Continue cutting until all the possible dough has been cut into circles **(A)**.

3. Dust the thicker bottom portion of the stamp lightly with flour, then one by one, place the dough "coins" onto the stamp. Dust the top with flour and press the dough coin firmly with the upper side of the stamp (with handle) to emboss the image **(B)**.

4. Release corzetti from the stamp and arrange them on a pasta drying rack, or a clean cloth or kitchen towels lightly dusted with flour.

5. Allow the corzetti to dry for 1 hour **(C)** before cooking in boiling salted water in a large, wide pot **(D)**. Serve with sage and pine nuts sizzled in butter and topped with grated cheese, basil and pine nut pesto, or *cicoria* (curly endive) and almond pesto.

NOTES: You will need rather thick sheets to emboss the design into the corzetti. Sometimes cooked, chopped borage leaves - *boraggio* in Italian and a favourite in Genoa - or chopped marjoram leaves are added to the dough for herbal flavour and green tint.

GARGANELLI

A SPECIALTY OF Emilia-Romagna, these hand-rolled hollow pasta shapes are shaped with a small ridged wooden board called a *pettine* (or comb) and its accompanying miniature rolling pin. The word "garganelli" comes from the Italian *garganeli*, meaning a chicken's gullet, and is related to the English word "gargle." The dough, which contains Parmigiano-Reggiano cheese native to the region and freshly grated nutmeg, a typical flavouring in Emilia-Romagna, should be firm but slightly moist so that it can form a good seal. Garganelli are often served in capon or rich chicken or meat broth or with Bolognese meat ragù. Or, make a sauce of puréed asparagus with a small amount of cream. Sauté asparagus tips and thin-sliced prosciutto strips, and toss with garganelli, asparagus sauce, and grated Parmigiano.

¾ pound (350 g) Italian 00 flour or unbleached all-purpose flour
Pinch fine sea salt
3 large eggs, at room temperature
2 ounces (2 handfuls, or 50 g) grated Parmigiano-Reggiano cheese
½ teaspoon freshly grated nutmeg

Yield: about 18 ounces (500 g), serves 5 to 6

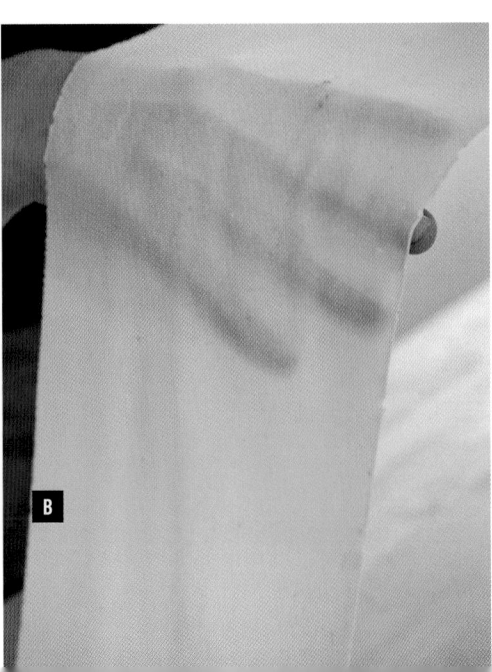

1. Place a mound of most of the flour (keeping about ½ cup, or 60 g, aside for rolling) on a wooden work surface or a large bowl. Sprinkle on the pinch of salt. Make a well in the centre and add the eggs. Using a fork, gradually work the flour into the egg mixture, then add the cheese and nutmeg. Push the wet dough that has accumulated off the fork into the dough **(A)**. Knead the dough until cohesive and moderately smooth, about 5 minutes, if using the pasta sheeter. If rolling by hand, knead until the dough is smooth and shiny, about 10 minutes.

2. Divide the dough into 4 or 5 sections, keeping all but 1 covered. Roll into a thin sheet with a sheeter or a large wooden rolling pin, dusting the sheet of pasta, the work surface, and the rolling pin lightly with the flour as needed. Dust with a minimum of flour because if the dough is too dry, the edges won't seal well **(B)**.

3. Cut the pasta into 2-inch (5-cm) squares, using a ridged adjustable cutter with two wheels or a knife: Use the adjustable cutter to make guidelines on the bottom edge of the pasta dough sheet. Cut 1 strip. Measure 2 inches (5 cm) and place the cutter to cut a second strip **(C)**. This way you won't be recutting the same portion of dough. Pull off the trimmings, cover, knead lightly to combine, and allow them to rest before rerolling if desired.

4. Place 1 pasta dough square on the diagonal onto the small ridged board. Use the miniature rolling pin to roll the pasta square onto the ridged "comb" **(D)**. Press the 2 pointed edges down firmly so they adhere.

5. Slide the completed garganelli from the pin **(E)**.

6. Arrange the garganelli on a mesh pasta drying rack or a lightly floured clean cotton cloth that has been dusted with semolina or cornmeal. Allow them to dry at least 30 minutes before cooking in broth or boiling salted water. Once dry, the garganelli keep well at room temperature for about 1 month if kept in a cool place with low humidity to prevent mold from forming.

C

D

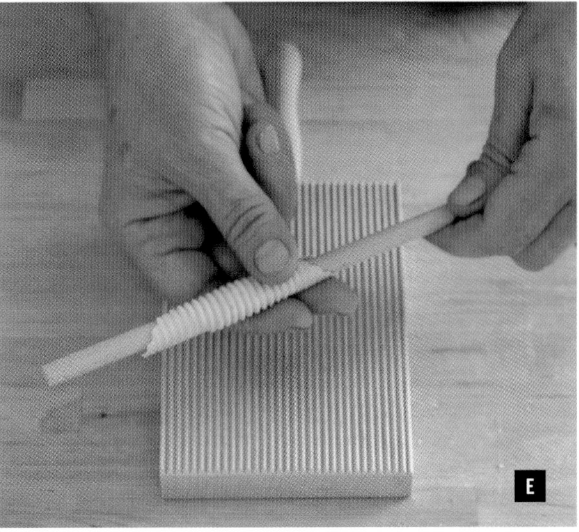
E

CHINESE CAT'S EAR NOODLES (MAO ER DUO)

THESE HAND-FORMED noodles from China resemble Italian orecchiette (little ears). Dough made from soft wheat flour dough is cut into little pillowy squares then pinched between thumb and forefinger to shape them into an ear-shaped cone. They are a famed street food snack in Hangzhou, China, stir-fried with a rich sauce. In Shanxi, which borders Inner Mongolia to the north and is famous for its black vinegar, "cat's ears" are stir-fried with pork, cabbage, soy, and vinegar and may be made with buckwheat flour.

1 pound (450 g) Japanese Udon Noodles dough (page 112), rested for at least 1 hour before rolling

Yield: about 1 pound (450 g), serves 4 to 6

A

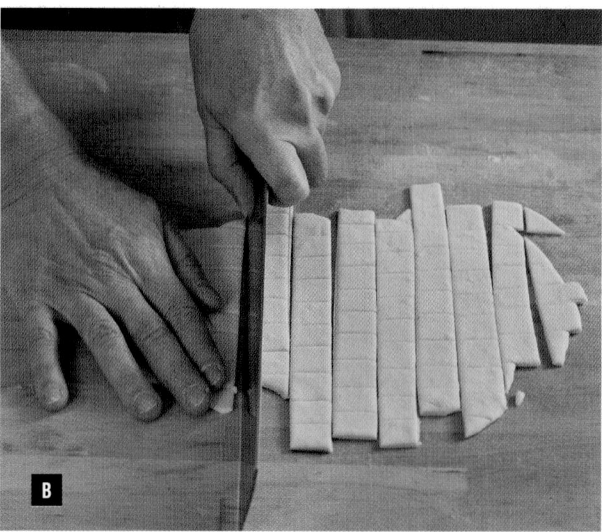

B

C

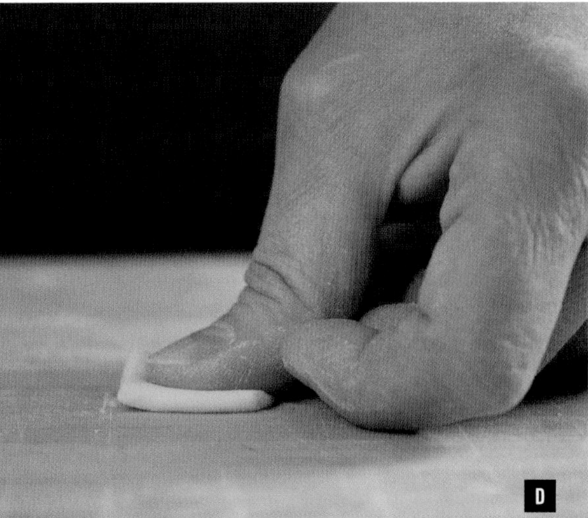
D

1. Sprinkle flour over a cutting board, preferably wood. Divide the dough into 2 sections. Place the dough on the board and roll it into a large rectangle about ¼ inch (6 mm) thick. Sprinkle more flour over the dough. Cut into even strips about ½ inch (1 cm) wide **(A)**. Repeat, cutting in the opposite direction to create small pillowy squares **(B)**.

2. Separate the squares and dust with flour **(C)**.

3. Using your thumb, flatten a square, pushing your thumb down and forward halfway between the centre and the edge so that the side curls up slightly into a cone shape **(D & E)**. (It will curl toward the right edge if you're right-handed, toward the left if left-handed.) Repeat until all the dough is finished.

   A completed cat's ear **(F)**.

4. As the cat's ears are shaped, arrange them on a mesh pasta drying rack so none are touching. If the dough is sticky or the weather is humid, toss the cat's ears lightly with extra flour, shaking off the excess. Cook the cat's ears while they are fresh and pliable in a large pot of salted boiling water until tender but chewy before tossing with desired sauce.

E

F

PUGLIESE ORECCHIETTE

THE NAME OF this hand-formed pasta means "little ears," which they resemble perfectly with their wrinkled surface and thicker rounded edges. They are the best-known form of *pasta strascinate*, pasta that is dragged - *strascinato* - across a wooden board by hand or using a knife or other utensil. Orecchiette may have arrived in Southern Italy from medieval Provence with the Angevin counts who dominated Puglia in the thirteenth century. In the nineteenth century, peasants would collect the leftover grains of wheat burnt by the hot steam engines used for harvesting. This "grano arso" was ground into flour and mixed with water, producing dark, smoky orecchiette. It is now an expensive artisanal regional specialty.

6 ounces (170 g) durum flour
6 ounces (170 g) semolina, plus extra for rolling
¾ cup (175 ml) warm water

Yield: 14 ounces (400 g), serves 4 to 5

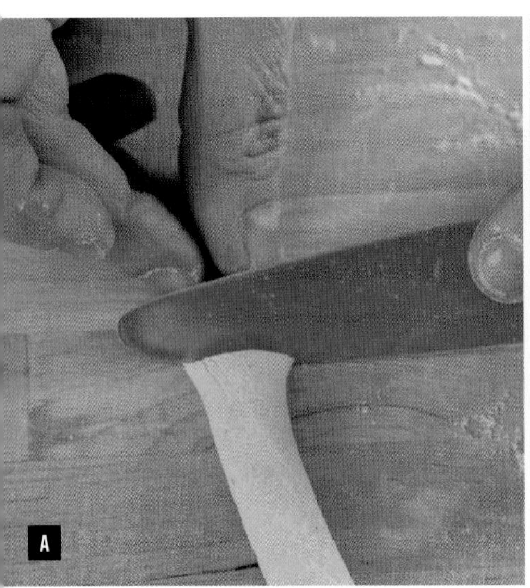

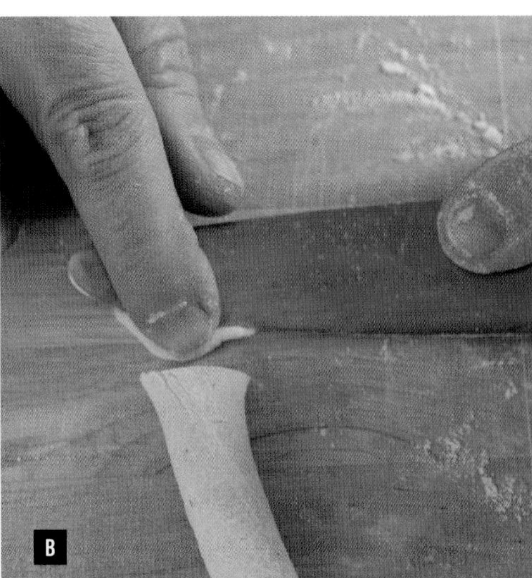

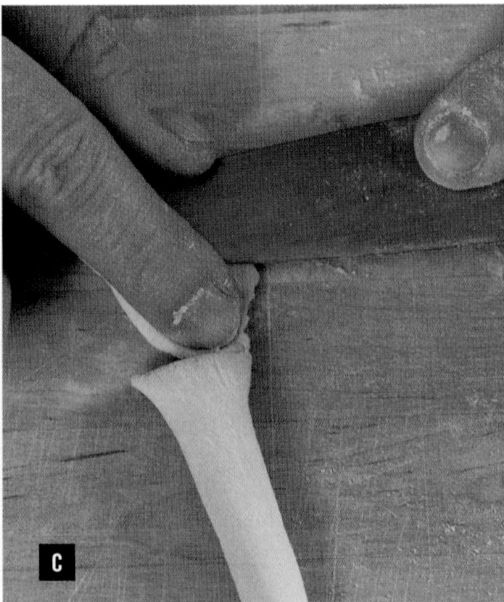

1. Mound both flours in a large bowl or on a wooden work surface, making a "volcano" with a "crater" in the centre.

2. Slowly pour in the water, whisking with a fork to incorporate the flour. Continue adding water and beating in the flour until a rough but cohesive dough is formed. Knead the dough until it is smooth and elastic, about 10 minutes. Cover with a bowl or plastic wrap and allow the dough to rest at least 1 hour to relax the gluten.

3. Divide the dough into 6 sections, keeping all but 1 covered with plastic wrap or a damp cloth. Roll 1 section into a rope about the thickness of a pencil.

4. Using a table knife (not a sharp chef's knife), cut the rope into a coin shape about ¼ inch (6 mm) thick **(A)**.

5. Angle the knife blade downward until it is almost flat on the surface **(B)**.

   Use the edge to drag the dough coin away from your body, scraping it along the table surface. Use the forefinger of your other hand to pin the edge of the coin down to the table while scraping away with the knife **(C & D)**. This forms the coin into a rough circle.

   A completed orecchiette disc **(E)**.

6. Flip the "dragged" piece of dough over your thumb to create a small "ear" with its rough inner surface now on the outside **(F)**.

   Repeat with the remaining dough, cutting and dragging 1 coin at a time until all the dough has been used.

7. As the orecchiette are completed, arrange them on a mesh pasta drying rack or a cotton cloth that has been lightly dusted with semolina. Keep the orecchiette from touching each other so they don't stick. Allow the orecchiette to dry at least 30 minutes before cooking in a large pot of salted boiling water until almost cooked through and still chewy, about 10 minutes.

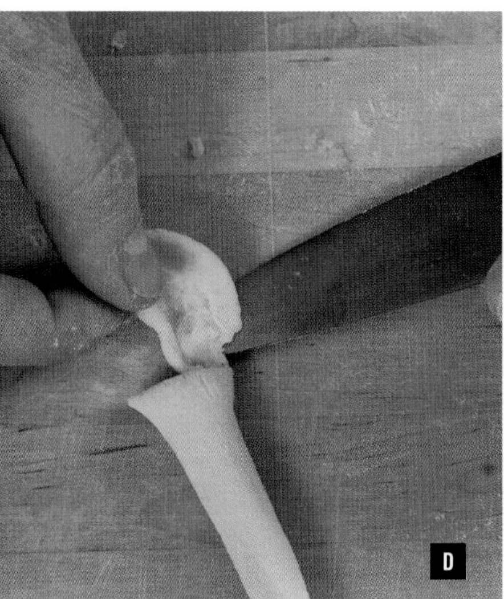
D

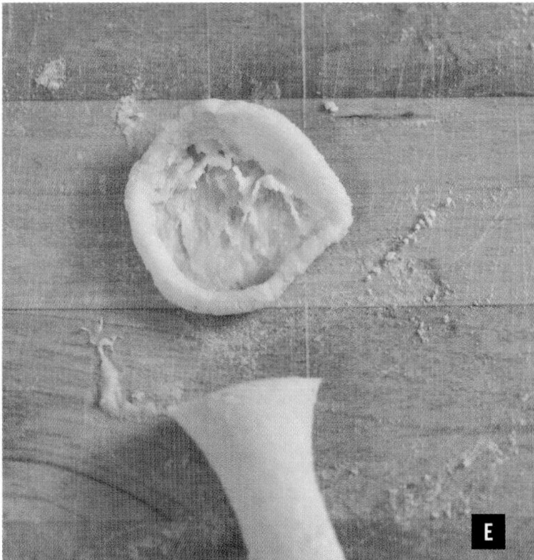
E

F

UMBRIAN OMBRICHELLI

THE NAME FOR these hand-formed strings of eggless dough literally means "earthworms." Ombrichelli are also known as pici, ghighi, and lombrichi and are most commonly found in the province of Viterbo in Lazio and nearby Orvieto in Umbria. Hearkening back to a time when eggs were a luxury, this pasta is made from a tender dough of soft wheat flour and water. Ombrichelli are usually served as pastasciutta (literally "dry" pasta) with a simple sauce of tomato, garlic, olive oil, and chile, or a meat ragù. They should be prepared and cooked the same day - ombrichelli get dry and brittle very quickly.

10 ounces (275 g) Italian 00 flour, unbleached all-purpose flour, or Korean flour, plus extra for rolling
5 ounces (150 ml) tepid water

Yield: about 15 ounces (425 g), serves 4 to 6

1 Mound the flour in the centre of a large wooden board or other work surface or in a large bowl to form a flour "volcano" with a "crater" in the middle. Pour the water into the crater, and, using a fork, begin to incorporate the flour, starting with the inner rim. Follow the directions in Basic Egg Pasta Dough on page 31 to complete the dough.

2 Pat the dough into a rough rectangle and cut into 4 sections. Cover all but 1 with plastic wrap. Place one section on a wooden work surface and dust with flour on both sides. Flatten the dough section with your hands, then use a wooden rolling pin, preferably the

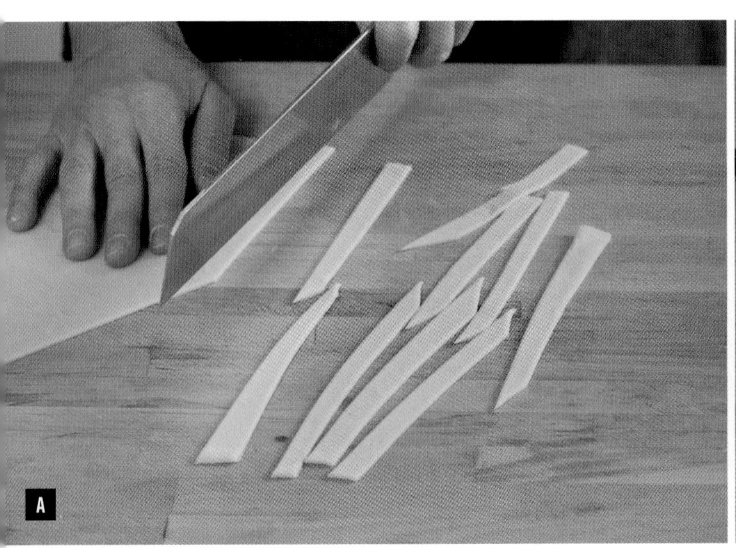

A

B

type without handles for more control, to roll it out into a roughly rectangular shape about ¼ inch (6 mm) thick.

3 Cut slices across the short end of the rectangle of roughly even thickness - each slice will become a single strand of dough **(A)**.

4 Pinch the edges of the strip toward the centre to form a thicker strand **(B)**.

5 Using the palms of your hands, roll 1 strip at a time from the centre toward the outside edges smoothly with light, even pressure as if you were working with modeling clay. Your object is to form thick relatively regular spaghettilike strands about 8 to 10 inches (20 to 25 cm) long with tapered, rather than bulbous, ends **(C–F)**.

6 Continue cutting slices and rolling the strips, dusting with flour before dropping into a loose pile. When you have a good-size pile (about enough for a serving), pick up the strands, dust with flour, and shake so they are all coated.

7 When the ombrichelli are complete, cook in well-salted boiling water until barely tender on the inside, 3 to 4 minutes. The ombrichelli will be tender but chewy. Drain and toss gently with simmering sauce.

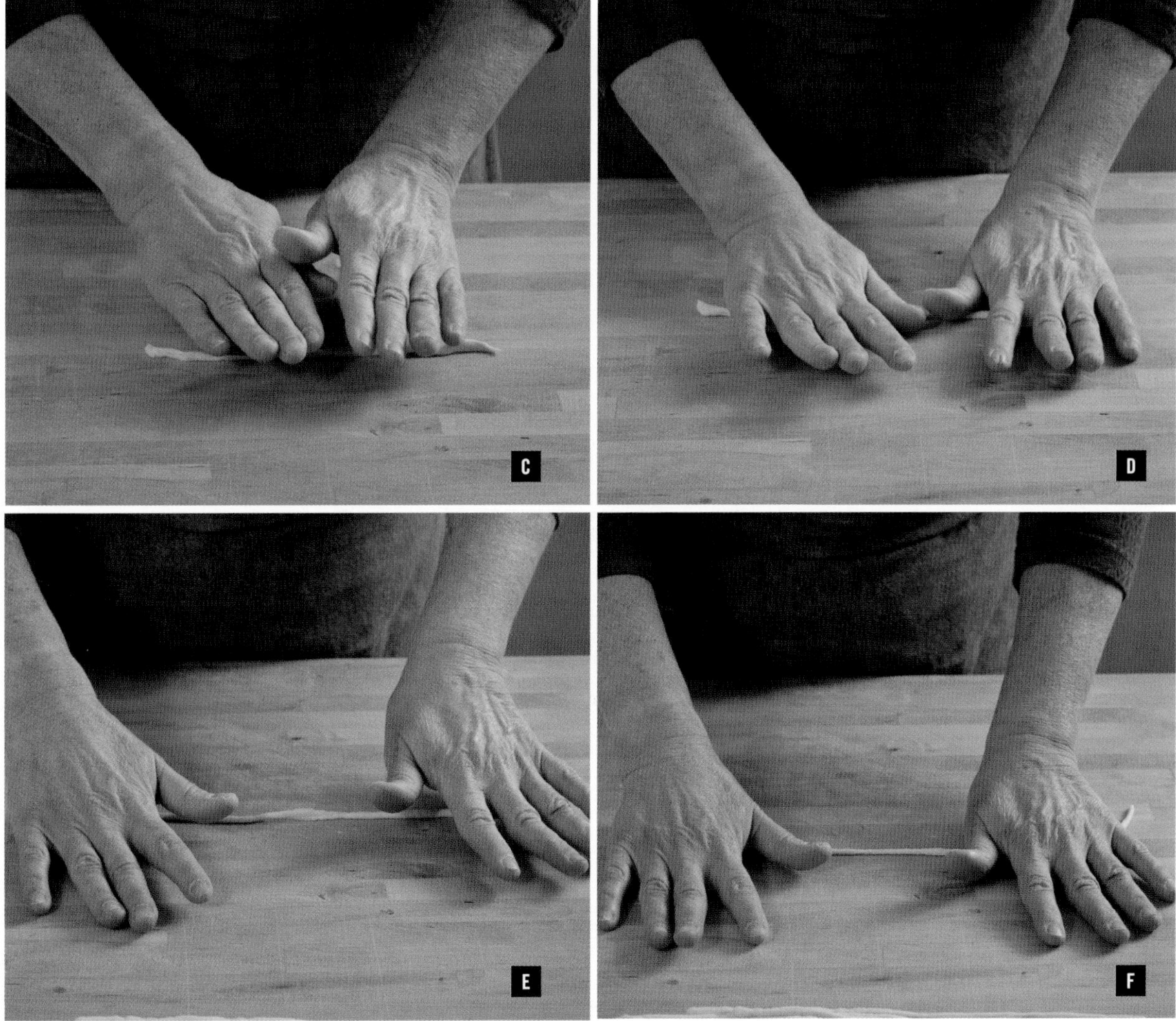
C
D
E
F

Trahana rolled in sheets and broken into small bits

Traditional grated trahana

GREEK TRAHANA

TRAHANA ARE SMALL, very hard bits of wheat flour or cracked wheat and yogurt dough mentioned in an eleventh-century Persian dictionary. They are found under similar names in Greece, Cyprus, Turkey, Iran, Albania, and Hungary and as *kishk* in Egypt and *kushuk* in Iraq. Trahana is traditionally prepared in summer and sun-dried, stored, then served in a thick wintertime soup. Because the dough is acidic and low in moisture, the milk proteins keep well for long periods of time. In this version from the Greek island of Chios, freely adapted from Aglaia Kremezi's *The Foods of the Greek Islands*, the dough includes yogurt, summer vegetables, and summer savory.

These are two methods among many of making the trahana. In my nontraditional way inspired by Italian technique, the dough is rolled out and dried in sheets then broken up with a mallet; the second is a traditional Greek technique in which the dough is patted into rounds, dried, and then grated.

1½ pounds (675 g), or 4 to 6 ripe tomatoes, cored and quartered, or canned chopped plum tomatoes in juice plus 1 cup (235 ml) water
¾ pound (350 g), or 2 sweet red bell peppers, cored, seeded, and diced
1 pound (450 g), or 2 large onions, peeled, cored, and coarsely chopped
2 large sprigs fresh savory or 1 tablespoon (3 g) crumbled dried savory
Sea salt to taste
1½ pounds (675 g) semolina
1 cup (235 g) thick Greek yogurt
1 pound (450 g) bread flour, plus extra if needed

Yield: 1½ pounds (675 g) dried trahana (2½ pounds, or 1.1 kg, before drying), serves 12 or more

1. In a large heavy-bottomed pot, combine the tomatoes, peppers, onions, savory, and a pinch of salt and bring to a boil. Reduce the heat to low, cover, and simmer until the vegetables are quite soft, about 30 minutes, stirring occasionally. If using fresh savory, remove and discard the sprigs.

2. Transfer the mixture to a blender or food processor and blend or process until fine.

3. Strain the vegetable mixture through a food mill to remove the fibres. (You should have about 4 cups of thick vegetable purée.) Transfer the mixture to a large bowl and let cool to room temperature.

4. Using a whisk, mix the semolina and salt to taste into the vegetable purée **(A)**. Cover with plastic wrap and allow the mixture to rest at room temperature for 30 minutes to absorb the semolina.

5. Line 6 large baking sheets with parchment paper, aluminum foil, or silicone baking mats.

6. Stir the yogurt into the vegetable mixture **(B)**. Beat in the bread flour making a soft dough that holds its shape.

7. Transfer the soft trahana dough to a wooden work surface. Dust with flour and knead 10 minutes or until smooth, adding more flour as necessary **(C & D)**.

A B C D

8 Preheat the oven to 200°F (93°C). A convection oven works well as does a bread warmer heated to low or a dehydrator.

9 Divide the dough into 6 pieces. Dust the work surface generously with flour and roll out each piece of dough into a rough rectangle about ¼ inch (6 mm) thick **(E)**.

10 Transfer to a baking sheet and continue with the remaining dough pieces **(F)**.

11 Allow the dough sheets to dry in the oven for 2 to 3 hours, turning them once after about 1 hour so they'll dry evenly **(G)**.

12 Turn the dough sheets over and bake again for 2 hours or until hard enough to crack into shards **(H)**. If necessary, bake 1 to 2 hours longer, or until they are hard.

13 Cool the dough sheets to room temperature, then break them into small pieces. Place the cracked bits onto the centre of a large kitchen towel, working in several batches if necessary. Cover with the sides of the towel folded over and, using a meat mallet or a hammer, bash the pieces repeatedly, breaking up the sheets into small crumb-size bits **(I)**.

14 If the dough bits are completely hard, they are ready to cook. If they are still moist and pliable, transfer them back to the baking pans and dry them in the oven 2 hours more, stirring the crumbs occasionally. Cool the trahana to room temperature then store in glass jars up to 6 months at room temperature, making sure they stay dry to avoid spoilage.

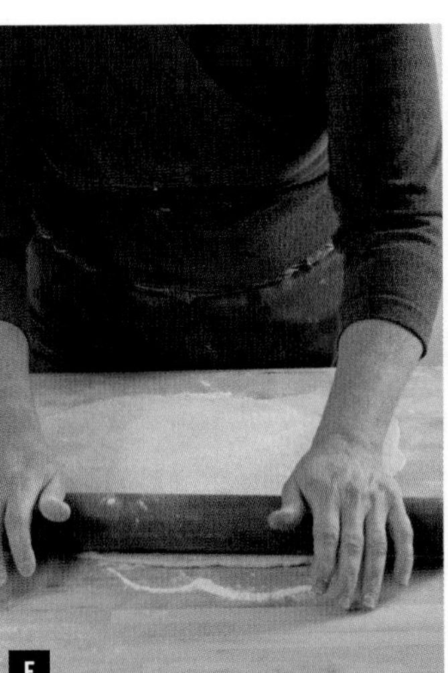
E

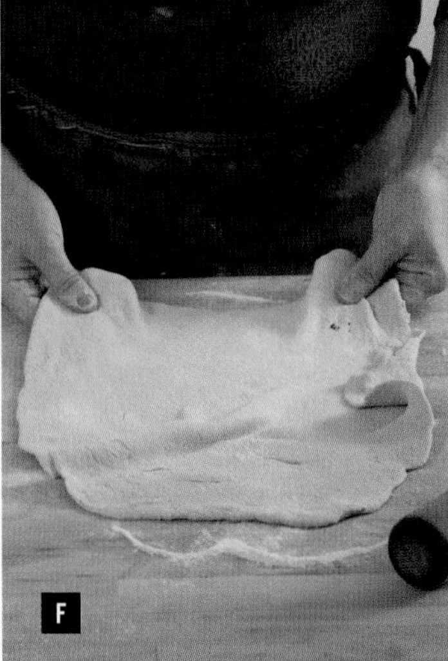
F

G

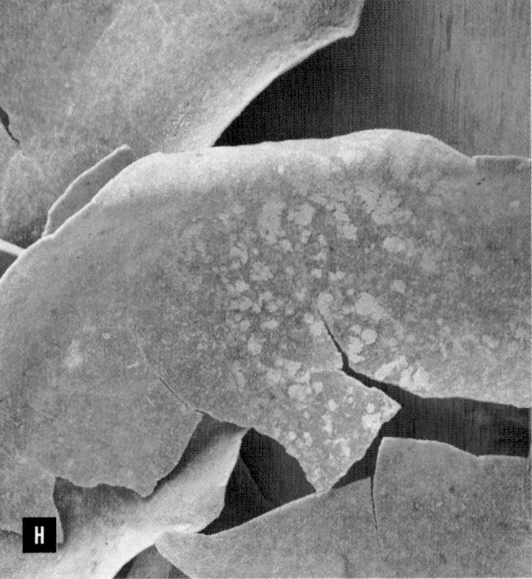
H

I

TRADITIONAL **GREEK METHOD**

1. Alternatively, work through step 7 **(D)**. Then continue with step 9, instead patting the sections of dough into fat rounds that resemble pita bread **(J)**.

2. Place the rounds on a baking tray lined with a silicone baking sheet or parchment paper, then bake at lowest heat in the oven (usually 175°F, or 80°C), or in a bread warmer on low for about 2 hours, turning once, or until the dough round is firm and leathery but not hard **(J)**. Remove from the oven and cool to room temperature.

3. Break the round in half, then grate against the large holes on the side of a box grater, forming large crumbs **(K)**.

4. Break up any larger bits by hand **(L)**. Spread the crumbs on a baking sheet and bake again at lowest heat in the oven, or in a bread warmer for 1 to 2 hours, or until the crumbs are hard and dry.

5. Remove from the oven and cool to room temperature before storing in a tightly sealed container, preferably glass, ceramic, or metal up to 6 months.

6. To cook the trahana, bring 2 quarts (1.9 L) flavourful chicken or vegetable broth to a boil, adding 1 cup (180 g) diced fresh tomatoes. Season with salt and Aleppo pepper flakes or hot red pepper flakes. Add 1 cup (225 g) of trahana and simmer until the pasta is soft, about 20 minutes. Stir in grated haloumi or crumbled feta cheese just before serving and garnish with chopped Italian parsley.

J

K

L

CHAPTER **EIGHT**

STUFFED PASTA

WHETHER POT STICKERS in China, pelmeni in Siberia, manti in Turkey, pierogi in Poland, kreplach in Jewish Eastern Europe, or the endless variations on ravioli (a word of mysterious origin) and tortelli (little cakes) in Italy, stuffed pasta pleases palates worldwide. Ravioli may have reached Italy through Sicily from the Arab world, as Iraqi sambusak, triangular pyramids of dough with a spiced ground meat filling, are mentioned in a thirteenth-century Italian compilation of Arab recipes. The earliest ravioli were dough stuffed with a filling, but by the early seventeenth century the filling cooked minus any dough covering became known as Ravioli Gnudi (page 72).

Stuffed pastas, or ravioli for simplicity, are more complex to prepare, but also quite satisfying as you can control filling ingredients, their consistency, and the type of dough used to wrap them. One of the big advantages of making your own stuffed pasta is that the machine-made product never contains as much filling and the dough, by necessity, must be firm and rolled thick to prevent breakage.

In this chapter, you'll learn to make ravioli using a plaque, to make tortelloni by hand, to make the small stuffed pasta squares or rings called tortellini, potato-stuffed Polish pierogi, and the closely related fruit-filled Ukrainian vareniki, as well as Chinese pot stickers, Genoese pansotti, Turkish manti, Siberian pelmeni, and a striking giant raviolo. Once stuffed, cook the ravioli right away; sprinkle with semolina to keep them separate, cover with plastic wrap, and refrigerate a day or two; or freeze (see page 137).

RAVIOLI TIPS

■ You are authorised to cut and paste to fill any holes in stuffed pasta. Dip your fingertip in water and dab it around the hole. Press a small bit of rolled-out dough over the hole - the wet dough will adhere. Cook as usual.

■ Fill your stuffed pasta as much as possible, which will make a tastier dish and will prevent air pockets that tend to puff up and split open when boiling the ravioli.

■ It is most important to prevent the filling from touching the rim of the dough, which will prevent the two layers of pasta dough from sticking together. Any filling on the edges will keep the dough layers from making a good seal, and the stuffed pasta will tend to open up while boiling.

■ When ready to stuff, cut each sheet into 2 equal sections. Place dollops of the stuffing along one sheet. Lightly mist the tops of both sections with water from a spray bottle to moisten, then cover the stuffed sheet with the second section: The moisture will help join the two. Don't mist before placing the stuffing because the small mounds will tend to slide around on the slick surface.

■ Poke a tiny hole in the centre of each raviolo or other stuffed pasta with a toothpick to help prevent it from bursting open when boiled.

TRADITIONAL PASTA-MAKING TOOLS

Shown above is a traditional Bolognese oak pasta rolling pin. On the hand-carved Italian olivewood cutting board are pasta cutting tools: From top left corner and going clockwise around the outside: spring-loaded brass cappelletti stamp with ejector **(A)**, Genoese two-part carved wood corzetti mold **(B)**, rolling pasta cutting wheel to make 2⅜-inch (6-cm) crimped-edge squares **(C)**, spring-loaded square ravioli cutter **(D)**, rolling pasta cutter wheel to make 2-inch (5-cm) circles **(E)**, bronze crimped pasta cutting wheel **(F)**, triangular ravioli cutter to make 2¾-inch (7-cm)–diameter Genoese pansotti **(G)**. In the centre, a pastry wheel for 2-inch (5-cm) square ravioli **(H)**, and a double-wheeled adjustable-width pasta cutter that cuts ridged strips 1 inch (2.5 cm) to 4¼ inches (11 cm) wide **(I)**.

HOW TO COOK RAVIOLI

Bring a large wide pot, such as a Dutch oven, of salted water to a boil. Add the ravioli one at a time into the water so as not to drop the temperature of the water below the boil and to keep them from sticking together. Meanwhile, bring your desired sauce to a boil in a wide skillet.

Bring the water back to a boil and cook at a moderate boil about 3 minutes, or until the edges are soft. Stir occasionally with a silicone spatula or wooden spoon so that the top and bottom sides cook evenly. (Cut the edge to check. You should see no white line of uncooked pasta dough running across the centre.) Using a slotted spoon or wire skimmer, remove the stuffed pasta from the water and add to the sauce, shaking the pan to coat the pasta with the sauce. The little bit of pasta water that clings to the ravioli will thin and bind the sauce with a small amount of starch washed off as the pasta cooked.

Note that any ravioli that break open while boiling should be discarded, as they will be full of water inside.

A large Chinese brass wire skimmer is ideal for scooping ravioli or other delicate pasta from the water. (See photo D on page 121 to see a Chinese brass wire skimmer in action.)

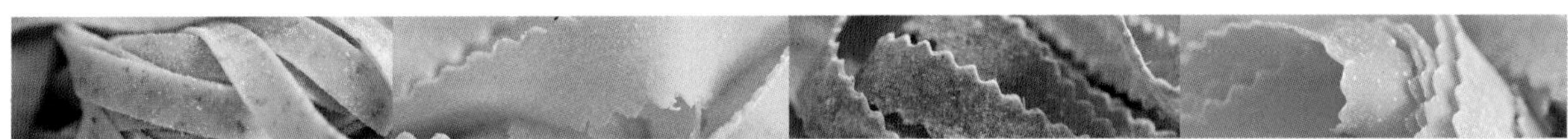

HOW TO FREEZE RAVIOLI AND OTHER STUFFED PASTA

Cover a tray with parchment paper or waxed paper that has been dusted lightly with semolina or cornmeal. Arrange the ravioli on the tray so none are touching. Place the tray in the freezer.

When the ravioli have frozen solid, gently remove them from the tray and transfer them to a heavy-duty freezer bag, or better yet, into a vacuum-sealable bag. Squeeze all the air from the bag or vacuum. Freeze pasta up to 1 month. If you have rolled the dough thin, the ravioli may crack and break open if vacuum-sealed. Instead, arrange frozen ravioli on a parchment paper– or waxed paper–lined flat box, such as a pizza box, in 2 or 3 layers with paper separating each layer. Overwrap the box in plastic wrap and freeze up to 1 month.

To cook frozen pasta: Add frozen ravioli one at a time directly to the pot of boiling water, allowing about 5 minutes of extra time for the pasta to cook through, especially on the edges where the dough is double-thick.

HOW TO REFRIGERATE RAVIOLI AND OTHER STUFFED PASTA

Especially in hot, humid weather, transfer ravioli to a tray lined with parchment or waxed paper and sprinkled with semolina or cornmeal, keeping them separate so they don't stick. Turn the ravioli over after 1 day so the bottoms stay dry. Cover the tray with plastic wrap and refrigerate up to 2 days before cooking.

MAKING RAVIOLI USING A PLAQUE

A RAVIOLI PLAQUE, or form, is a simple tool with two parts. Its metal top contains anywhere from 10 to 48 square ravioli openings with a raised, ridged cutting edge bordering each opening. The second part is a metal or plastic tray with a corresponding number of smaller circular pockets used to press an indentation inside each ravioli square to contain the filling.

Here I make goat cheese–stuffed ravioli in the style of Provence, France, enclosed in roasted red pepper pasta.

GOAT CHEESE FILLING

11 to 12 ounces (310 to 340 g) fresh mild goat cheese (1 log is often 11 ounces)
¾ cup (175 g) whole milk ricotta or farmers' cheese
½ cup (25 g) fresh white bread crumbs (if using ricotta)
2 egg yolks
2 tablespoons (5 g) minced basil, dill, or tarragon (or a combination of all 3)
2 tablespoons (6 g) thinly sliced chives
¼ cup (40 g) finely diced red onion
Freshly ground black pepper and pinch fine sea salt
1 batch Roasted Red Pepper Pasta Dough (page 50)

Yield: about 48 ravioli (using a plaque that makes 12 ravioli per batch), serves 8 as an appetizer or 6 as a main dish

1 Combine the goat cheese, ricotta or farmers' cheese, bread crumbs (if using), egg yolks, herbs, red onion, black pepper, and a pinch of salt in a medium bowl. Beat together using a wooden spoon or a heavy whisk until well-combined and no goat cheese lumps remain. Reserve. (You may store the filling covered and refrigerated for up to 2 days before filling the ravioli.)

SHAPE THE RAVIOLI:

2 Cut the dough into lengths about 1 inch (2.5 cm) longer then the ravioli plaque, usually 2 sheets per rolled-out section of dough **(A)**.

3 Place a length of dough on a lightly floured ravioli plaque. Use the metal tray to press down so that the dough adheres to the plaque while forming cup-shaped indentations in each square **(B & C)**.

4 Pipe or spoon the filling into each depression, making sure to keep the filling away from the borders and filling as much as possible **(D)**. If the dough is dry, use a small brush or your fingers dipped in water to lightly brush water along the edges of each ravioli square so the top layer will adhere. Filling the depressions fully will prevent air pockets that tend to puff up and split open when boiling the ravioli.

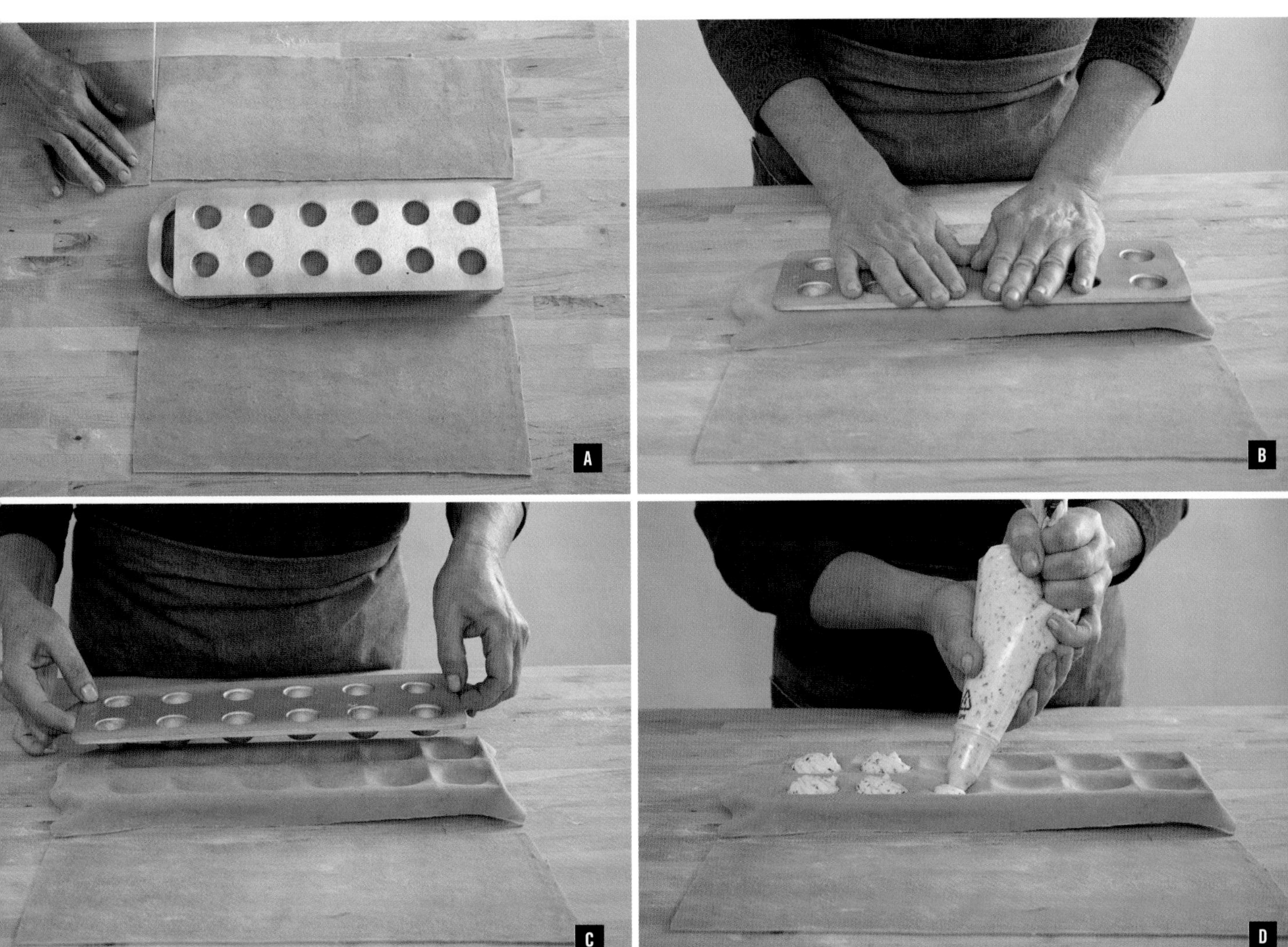

E

F

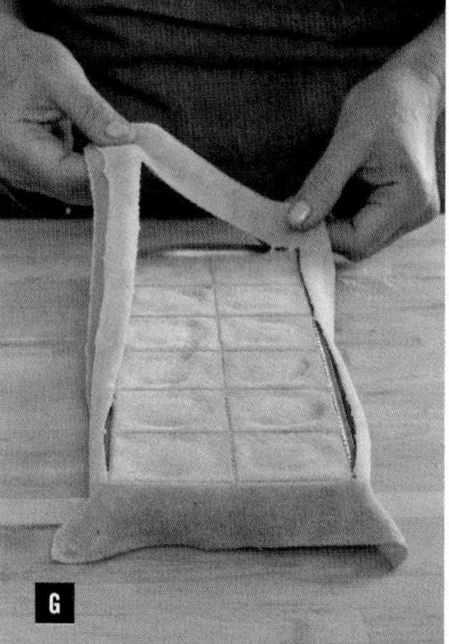
G

H

5 Cover the filled ravioli with a second sheet of pasta dough **(E)**.

6 Using a rolling pin, roll back and forth and side to side to join the two layers of dough and seal the ravioli edges. Turn the rolling pin on a 45-degree angle and roll back and forth, pressing down firmly on the pin to cut through the dough **(F)**. Turn the pin 90 degrees and repeat. The edges should be mostly cut through and the individual ravioli should be mostly freed from the excess dough.

7 Remove the excess dough from the edges **(G)**, wrapping and saving the excess for another use, if desired.

8 Turn the ravioli plaque upside down over a mesh pasta drying rack or a lightly floured board so the ravioli release **(H)**. Gently separate any ravioli that are still joined, using a sharp knife or ravioli wheel (preferably ridged) to cut between the individual ravioli pillows. Continue making ravioli until all the filling and dough has been used.

9 Arrange the ravioli on a mesh pasta drying rack or a clean towel or cloth that has been dusted with semolina or cornmeal. Turn the ravioli over after about 30 minutes so the bottoms do not get sticky. Ideally, cook the ravioli within 2 hours of making them. Or, refrigerate or freeze them following the instructions on page 137.

The red pepper–goat cheese ravioli are ready to cook.

NOTE: If you wish (and little to no filling is mixed in), cover the dough trimmings with plastic wrap and allow them to rest before rolling out again. Because they were dusted with flour while rolling out, the trimmings will be dryer and better suited to making cut pasta rather than stuffed pasta.

TORTELLONI

THESE HAND-FORMED tortelloni from Emilia-Romagna are a classic made with substantial Swiss chard leaves, though spinach is often used instead. Though it is nontraditional, I like to use smoked mozzarella; you may substitute fresh for a more delicate flavour. Serve with Rose Sauce, page 119, for an exquisite combination.

½ pound (225 g) Swiss chard, ribs and large stems removed, leaves washed
1 container (15 ounces, or 425 g) container fresh thick whole milk ricotta cheese, drained if at all watery
Freshly grated nutmeg to taste
Salt and black pepper to taste
¼ cup (40 g) grated smoked mozzarella
¼ cup (25 g) grated Parmigiano Reggiano cheese or Grana Padano
1 batch Three-Egg Basic Pasta Dough (page 30)

Yield: about 36 tortelloni, serves 4 to 6

PREPARE THE FILLING:

1 Heat a skillet with about 1 inch (2.5 cm) of water to boiling. Cook the chard for 2 to 3 minutes, or until wilted and softened but still deep green. Drain and then run under cold water to chill and set the colour. Gather the leaves in a ball in your hands and squeeze to remove most of the water. Finely chop the chard. (You should have about ½ cup, or 75 g.)

2 Mix together the chard, ricotta, several gratings of nutmeg, salt, pepper, smoked mozzarella, and grated cheese. The filling should be mostly white with abundant flecks of green, smooth, well-seasoned, and not at all watery.

FILL THE TORTELLONI:

3 Have ready a wooden work counter dusted with flour or a table lined with a cotton tablecloth, which will absorb just the right amount of moisture so the dough doesn't stick. Divide the dough into 4 sections and roll out one at a time using the pasta sheeter. Cut each roll into 2 individual sheets to make them easier to handle. Don't roll out to the thinnest setting; generally rolling to the next-to-last or second-to-last setting is sufficient.

A

B

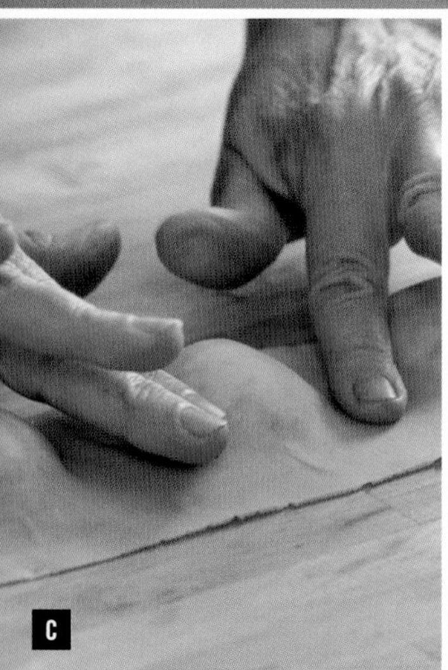
C

D

4 Fold the dough sheet in half lengthwise and run your fingers along the folded edge to mark the border, creating a guideline for placement of the filling dollops **(A)**.

5 Place heaping tablespoons (15 g) of the filling formed into balls in a row down the lengthwise centre of the dough strip, allowing about 1½ inches (4 cm) between each ball of filling **(B)**.

6 Grasp the edges of the dough on the long side farthest from you and bring up over the filling to meet the opposite edge. The balls of filling will roll over at the same time. Gently tap both edges together to make sure they meet evenly.

7 Now comes an important step: Push the dough down around the balls of filling while at the same time pushing out any air pockets, which can cause the finished tortelloni to break open. Go back over the dough, pressing the sealed edges to thin them so the tortelloni will cook evenly and to ensure they are well-sealed **(C)**.

8 Using a ridged pasta cutting wheel, trim off the excess dough lengthwise, leaving a ¼- to ½-inch (½- to 1-cm) border between the edge of the dough and the edge of the filling. Now slice across the dough to cut the tortelloni, discarding excess dough **(D)**. Repeat the process until all the dough has been rolled out and all the filling used.

9 Arrange the finished tortelloni on a wire screen or a wooden cutting board that has been dusted with semolina or cornmeal. Allow the tortelloni to dry at room temperature for about 30 minutes. In hot, humid weather, dry the tortelloni by placing them in front of a fan on low speed. Turn the tortelloni over after about 30 minutes to ensure that the moist filling doesn't stick to the mesh. The tortelloni are now ready to cook, refrigerate, or freeze.

TORTELLINI

BOLOGNA AND MODENA are rivals in claiming to be the birthplace of tortellini. These famous stuffed pasta rings are filled with a finely chopped mixture of cured meats, ground pork and/or veal, Parmigiano cheese, and nutmeg and are shaped from circles or squares of dough. If made from squares, they are also known as cappelletti - or little hats. The precious mouthfuls are cooked and served in meat, chicken, or, especially, capon broth.

¼ pound (115 g) prosciutto including its white fat, preferably in a single thick slice, diced and frozen until firm
¼ pound (115 g) mortadella, preferably in a single thick slice, diced and frozen until firm
1 large egg, at room temperature
½ teaspoon freshly grated nutmeg
Freshly ground black pepper to taste
¼ pound (115 g) grated Parmigiano-Reggiano cheese or Grana Padano
6 ounces (170 g) soft white or wheat bread without crust, crumbled
½ cup (115 g) unsalted butter
½ pound (225 g) ground pork
2 tablespoons (8 g) chopped Italian parsley
1 batch Three-Egg Basic Pasta Dough (page 30), preferably made with Italian 00 flour for silky texture, or All-Yolk Pasta Dough (page 30) for richness and firm bite

Yield: 2½ pounds (1.1 kg), serves 10 to 12

PREPARE THE FILLING:

1. Combine the prosciutto and mortadella in the bowl of a food processor and grind until fine but lightly chunky. Transfer to a mixing bowl and mix in the egg, nutmeg, black pepper, and cheese. Place the bread in the processor and process until fine, keeping separate from the meat.

A

B

C

2 In a large heavy-bottomed saucepan, heat the butter until it sizzles. Add the ground pork and brown over high heat, stirring occasionally. Add the ground prosciutto mixture and cook for 5 minutes more, breaking up with a wooden spoon. Remove from heat and allow to cool.

3 Transfer to a bowl and combine with bread crumbs and parsley. Place the mixture back in the processor and process until fine but not pasty. Cool then chill until ready to use, up to 2 days ahead, or wrap tightly or vacuum seal and freeze up to 1 month.

MAKE THE PASTA AND ASSEMBLE:

4 Using a pasta machine or rolling by hand, roll out the pasta until quite thin but not transparent, usually the next-to-last setting.

5 Cut the dough into 2-inch (5-cm) circles or squares **(A)**. (Don't cut too many circles or squares at once because they will dry out quickly. Keep the uncut dough covered with a damp cloth while forming the tortellini.)

6 Place 1 generous teaspoon of the tortellini filling in the centre of each circle or square **(B)**. Take care not to get any filling on the edges of the dough because it will prevent the dough from forming a good seal.

7 If the dough is too dry to form a good seal, brush with water or mist with water from a spray bottle *after* placing the filling **(C)**.

8 If using circles, fold them in half to make a half-moon shape, joining the top edges first **(D)**. (If using squares, arrange them on the diagonal, then pull the near edge of the dough over the filling and press the edges together to form a triangle starting at the top point.)

For both shapes, push out the excess air and press the edges together firmly to seal **(E)**.

9 Bring the half-moon or long triangle points together over your forefinger, forming a ring **(F)**. Press the points firmly to join them together and thin the dough for even cooking **(G)**.

10 Continue filling and shaping the tortellini until all the pasta and filling are used. Arrange the filled tortellini on a mesh pasta drying rack or a clean cotton cloth that has been sprinkled lightly with semolina or cornmeal to prevent sticking. Cover with a clean slightly damp towel to keep the pasta from hardening. Either cook immediately or cover and store refrigerated up to 3 days.

TRUE AND AUTHENTIC TORTELLINO

In 1974, the Bologna section of the Accademia Italiana della Cucina registered the ingredients and quantities of the "true and authentic" tortellino. Here is the recipe, enough to fill 1,000 tortellini: 300 grams pork loin browned in butter, 300 grams prosciutto crudo (Parma-style cured ham), 300 grams mortadella; 450 grams Parmigiano-Reggiano; 3 hen's eggs; and 1 nutmeg, grated.

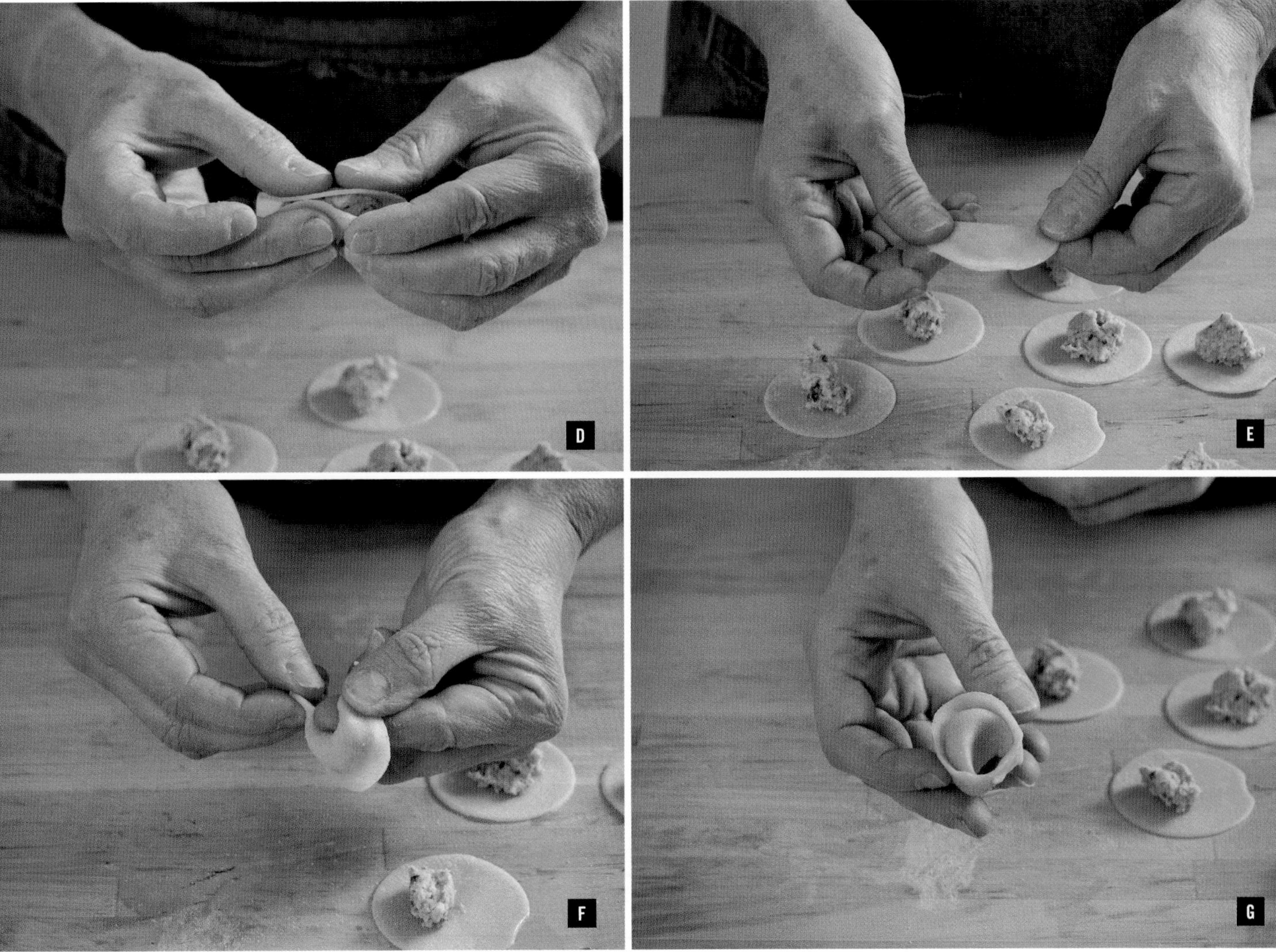

CARAMELLE

THIS AMUSING pasta resembles caramel candies wrapped in cellophane. The flavour and colour of the squash pasta complement the sweet potato filling. To show off their candylike shape, toss the caramelle in a simple sauce of butter cooked with sage leaves until the bits of milk solids are browned and nutty and sprinkle with cheese.

SWEET POTATO CARAMELLE

1½ pounds (675 g) sweet potatoes, preferably firm yellow-fleshed Northern American sweet potatoes such as Hayman
¾ cup (40 g) soft bread crumbs
2 ounces (55 g), or about ¾ cup, grated Parmigiano-Reggiano cheese or Grana Padano
2 egg yolks
Kosher salt, grated nutmeg, and freshly ground black pepper to taste
1 batch Squash Pasta Dough (see page 55) or 1 batch Three-Egg Basic Pasta Dough (page 30)
Extra flour for rolling

Yield: about 2 pounds (900 g), serves 6 to 8

A

B

1 Preheat the oven to 400°F (200ºC, or gas mark 6). Bake the sweet potatoes about 1 hour, or until tender when pierced. Remove from the oven, cool, and then peel. Mash the sweet potato with the remaining ingredients and chill in the refrigerator.

2 To form the caramelle, roll out the pasta dough into sheets. Cut each sheet into 2½ x 2½-inch (6 x 6-cm) squares using the adjustable ridged cutter **(A)**.

3 Transfer the filling to a piping bag fitted with a large plain tip or a resealable freezer bag with a ⅜-inch (1-cm) opening cut from one corner. Working with about 12 squares at a time, arrange them in rows all facing the same direction.

Pipe a 1-inch (2.5-cm) strip (like toothpaste) across each square, leaving a ¼ to ½-inch (6 mm to 1 cm) border all around **(B)**.

4 Fold up the bottom edge of the square, then overlap the top edge over the bottom for a secure joint that will prevent the filling from leaking out **(C & D)**. Press down to seal well. (If the dough is on the dry side, brush the top edge lightly with water before folding over.)

5 Twist the 2 ends of each caramella, then pinch at the joint so that the dough is not overly thick **(E & F)**.

A completed caramella **(G)**.

6 Arrange the completed caramelle on a mesh pasta drying rack or a clean cotton cloth that has been dusted lightly with semolina or cornmeal. Allow the caramelle to dry somewhat, turning them after about 30 minutes so their surface is evenly dried on all sides. Either cook the same day, refrigerate for up to two days, or freeze for another day, following the directions on page 137.

C

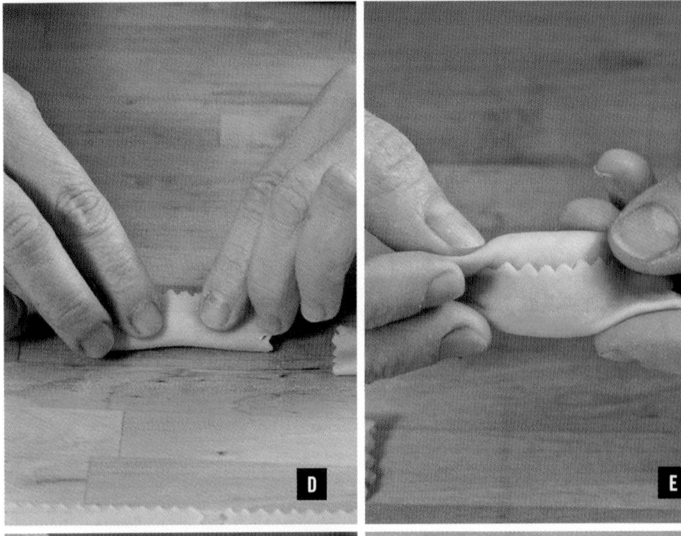
D E

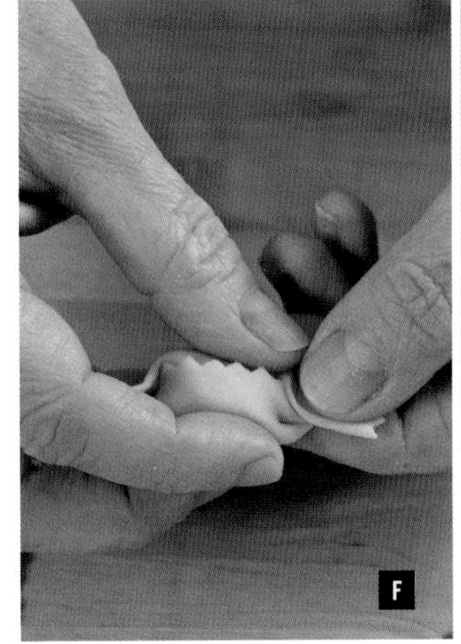
F

G

PIEROGI

PIEROGI ARE half-moon–shaped dumplings from Poland made from a rich elastic dough that usually includes sour cream or cream cheese. They may be filled with mashed potatoes (often flavoured with caramelised onions and/or grated Cheddar cheese), tangy white farmers' cheese, wild mushrooms, sauerkraut, and meat. Ukrainian vareniki (see page 154) are closely related. Pierogi are boiled, drained, and often fried in butter before serving with more melted butter and sour cream, or with fried bacon bits, onions, or mushrooms. The origin of the word "pierogi" is obscure. The root "pir" is found in many Slavic languages but usually means "pie."

GOLD POTATO AND CARAMELISED ONION PIEROGI FILLING

2 pounds (900 g), or 4 to 6 medium, Yukon gold or other gold potatoes
1 large egg, at room temperature
¼ cup (55 g) unsalted butter
1 pound (450 g), or 2 to 3 medium yellow onions, diced
½ pound (225 g) small-curd cottage cheese (drained) or farmers' cheese
1 teaspoon paprika
Sea salt and freshly ground black pepper to taste

Yield: about 3 pounds (1.4 kg), serves 12

1 Bring a large pot of salted water to a boil. Add the whole potatoes and cook until tender but not mushy, about 15 minutes. (Don't peel the potatoes before boiling as they will absorb too much water.) Drain and, when cool enough to handle, peel off the skin. Put the potatoes through a ricer or food mill while still hot. Transfer to a mixing bowl and beat in the egg.

2 Meanwhile, melt the butter in a medium-large heavy-bottomed skillet and add the onions. Cook over moderate heat until they give off their juices, about 10 minutes. Raise the heat and continue to cook until the onions are well-browned, about 15 minutes, stirring often. Remove from the heat and combine with the potato mixture, cottage cheese, and paprika. Season generously with salt and pepper, noting that the potatoes will absorb salt as they rest. Cool to room temperature or chill up to 2 days before using to fill the pierogi. (Any extra filling may be frozen for later use.)

PIEROGI DOUGH

4 ounces (115 g) cream cheese
1 large egg, at room temperature
1 teaspoon fine sea salt
2 tablespoons (30 ml) warm water
½ pound (225 g) unbleached all-purpose flour, plus extra for rolling

Yield: about 1 pound (450 g), serves 12

1 Place the cream cheese, egg, and salt in the bowl of a standing mixer or a food processor. Beat with the paddle or process until the mixture is smooth. Add the water and mix again until smooth.

2 Add the flour and beat or process until the mixture forms a cohesive mass that comes away from the sides of the bowl **(A & B)**.

3 Remove the dough from the machine and knead on a flour-dusted work surface until the dough is shiny, elastic, and no longer sticky, about 5 minutes. Cover with a bowl, a damp cloth, or plastic wrap and allow it to rest at room temperature for at least 30 minutes or up to overnight (refrigerated) to relax the gluten. (If refrigerating, allow the dough to come to room temperature before proceeding.)

4 Divide the dough into 4 sections, covering 3 of them to keep them moist. Dust a work board or counter with flour and, using a rolling pin, roll out the dough until you can just start to see the grain of the wood underneath, about ⅛ inch (3 mm) thick - about twice as thick as for ravioli because the dough is quite tender.

5 To make the pierogi with a metal form, cut the rolled-out dough into strips about 1 inch (2.5 cm) bigger in all directions than the size of the form **(C)**.

6 Lay a sheet of pierogi dough onto the flour-dusted metal form **(D)**.

7 Spoon the filling into the centres of each semicircle, shaping the filling into a roughly semicircular shape and keeping the filling from touching the edges, to form a good seal. **(E)**.

8 Cover with a second sheet of dough and press down with your fingers to join the 2 sheets **(F)**.

9 Roll over the top sheet with a rolling pin, back and forth and from side to side, to join the sheets and cut out the individual dumplings **(G)**. Remove the excess dough, saving it, covered to prevent drying out, for rerolling.

10 Turn the form upside down to release the pierogi **(H)**.

11 Prick each pierogi once in the centre of the stuffing portion with a toothpick to help prevent it from bursting open in boiling water.

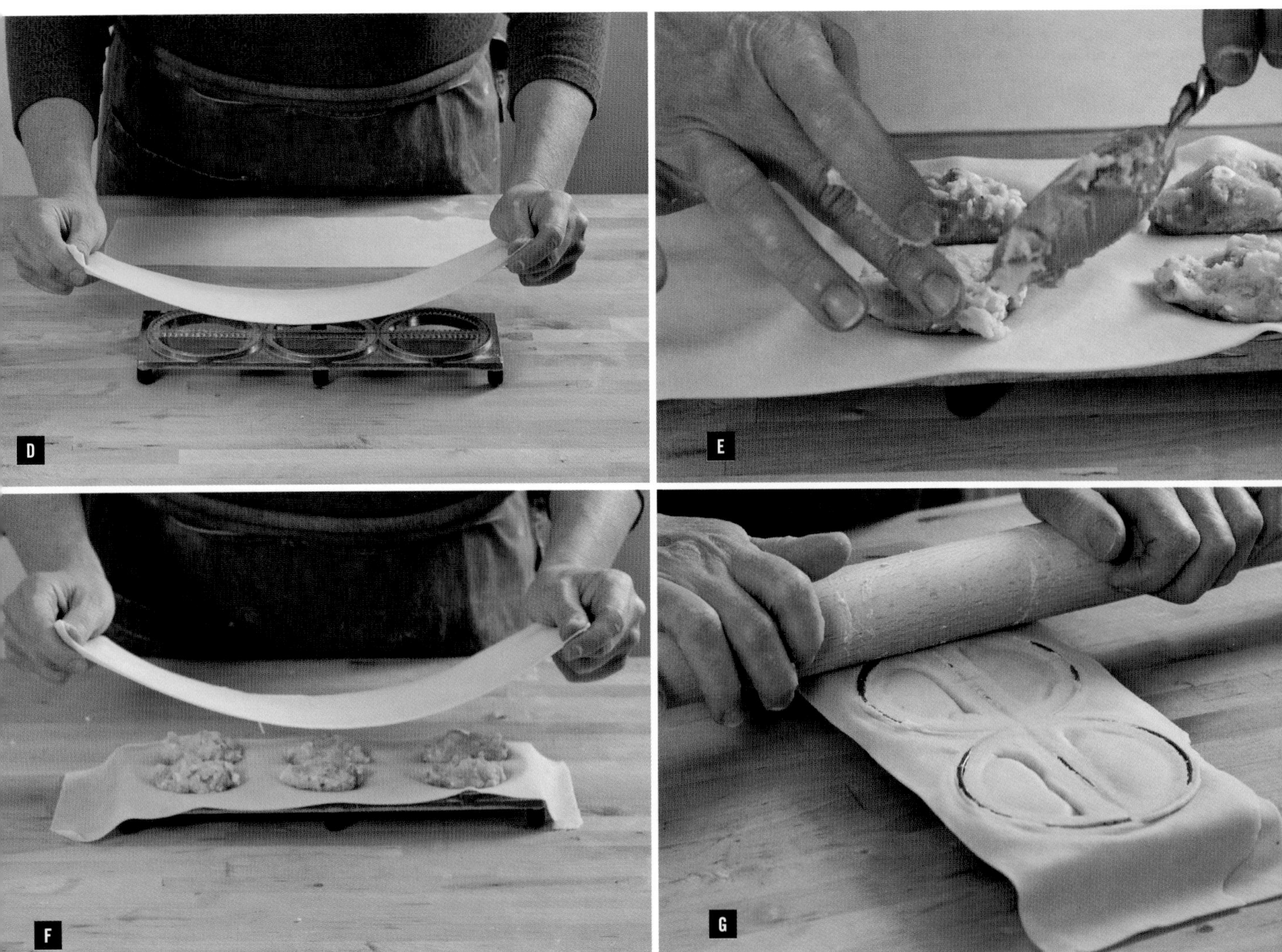
D E F G

12 Arrange the filled pierogi on a mesh pasta drying rack or a cotton tablecloth that has been dusted with semolina or cornmeal and allow them to dry up to 1 hour before cooking. (In humid weather, turn the pierogi over about 30 minutes so the bottoms don't stick.) Or, freeze according to the directions on page 137.

COOK THE PIEROGI:

13 Bring a large pot of salted water to a boil. Add the pierogi, a few at a time so that the temperature of the water doesn't drop below the boil. The pierogi will sink to the bottom at first. Once they rise to the top, cook for 3 or 4 minutes, or until they are tender at the edges. Scoop the pierogi from the water using a wire skimmer or slotted spoon.

14 Serve topped with melted butter and small dollops of sour cream or crispy bacon bits. Alternatively, heat oil in a large skillet, preferably nonstick, over medium-high heat. Fry the pierogi until browned and slightly crispy and serve with caramelised onions and mushrooms.

VARIATION: SHAPING PIEROGI BY HAND

Cut out circles of dough using a 3½-inch (9-cm)–diameter glass or cookie cutter. Repeat with remaining dough until all the circles have been cut out. (You may use the scraps and reroll them, covering and allowing them to rest for at least 1 hour to relax the gluten. This time use the pasta sheeter as the dough will be much firmer after being rolled the first time.) You should end up with about 64 circles.

Form the filling into 1½-inch (4-cm) balls, and place a ball slightly below the centre of a dough circle. Holding a circle in your hand, stretch the dough slightly to cover the filling and pinch the edges firmly to form a well-sealed crescent. If the filling squeezes out, you have filled the pierogi too much.

PORK, NAPA CABBAGE, AND GINGER POT STICKER FILLING

1 pound (450 g) ground pork (substitute ground dark meat turkey or duck)
1 bunch scallions, thinly sliced
¼ cup (60 ml) soy sauce
1 tablespoon (15 ml) toasted sesame oil
1 tablespoon (8 g) grated fresh ginger
3 cups shredded Napa cabbage (about ½ pound, or 225 g)
1-pound (455 g) package round gyoza skins

Yield: about 50 pot stickers, serves 6 to 8

POT STICKERS

THE CHINESE have been perfecting the art of dumpling for about 1,000 years. Their Chinese name, *jiaozi*, means "horn-shaped." During the Spring Festival that marks the start of a new year, people eat jiaozi to symbolise their wishes for good fortune. The half-moon stuffed dumplings have a ground meat and/or vegetable filling enclosed in a thin circle of soft wheat dough made with boiling water for greater elasticity. The dough circle is folded over and pinched into pleats by hand or by using a dumpling mold, then sealed by pressing the edges firmly together. The dough is available at Chinese and Asian markets in prerolled, precut circles under the name Shanghai dumpling wrappers, or their Japanese name, gyoza, as is the dumpling form.

Browned in a small amount of oil and then boiled by adding water to the cooking pan, pot stickers develop a pleasing, chewy texture with a crispy, well-browned side that sticks lightly to the pan. (They may also be deep-fried or steamed.) Jiaozi are traditionally served with the pan-fried side on top accompanied by soy-vinegar dipping sauce.

Here, we make pot stickers with purchased dumpling dough rounds, which are available in many supermarkets and Asian groceries.

1 In a large bowl, combine the pork, scallions, soy sauce, sesame oil, and ginger. Mix well so the meat absorbs the flavours. Add the cabbage and mix again. Refrigerate until ready to fill.

2 Have ready a pleated plastic or metal dumpling form, a small bowl containing 2 tablespoons (30 ml) egg white mixed with 1 tablespoon (15 ml) water, and the gyoza skins, defrosted overnight in refrigerator if necessary. Lay a dumpling wrapper into the form **(A)**.

3 Spoon 1 tablespoon (15 ml) of filling on each skin, making sure to keep the filling off the edges or they won't stick **(B)**. Brush the edge of the skin with the egg white mixture. (Or, simply brush with water, especially if the dough is moist.)

4 Grasping the gyoza by the edge, fold over and press the edges together using your fingertips **(C)**.

5 Grasping the handle, bring the far edge of the form over and press firmly to seal and form the "pleated" edge **(D)**.

6 Arrange the completed dumplings in a single layer on a parchment paper–lined baking tray that has been sprinkled lightly with cornstarch. Cover lightly with plastic wrap and refrigerate until ready to cook (up to 1 day if turned over once or twice to prevent sticking). Or, freeze following the directions on page 137.

COOK AND SERVE THE POT STICKERS:

7 Heat a large heavy-bottomed or nonstick skillet, preferably with a lid, until very hot. Add 1 tablespoon (15 ml) oil and swirl so the oil coats the bottom of the pan. Place the dumplings in a single layer in the pan, working in 2 batches. Sauté until the bottoms are golden brown, about 2 minutes, then add ½ cup (120 ml) of water to the pan.

8 Cover with a lid or a sheet of aluminum foil and cook 7 to 8 minutes, or until the water has evaporated, the dumplings are tender, and the bottoms are well-browned, shaking occasionally to release the dumplings from the pan. Repeat with the remaining dumplings. Serve with Soy Ginger Dipping Sauce, below, garnished with scallions and cilantro sprigs.

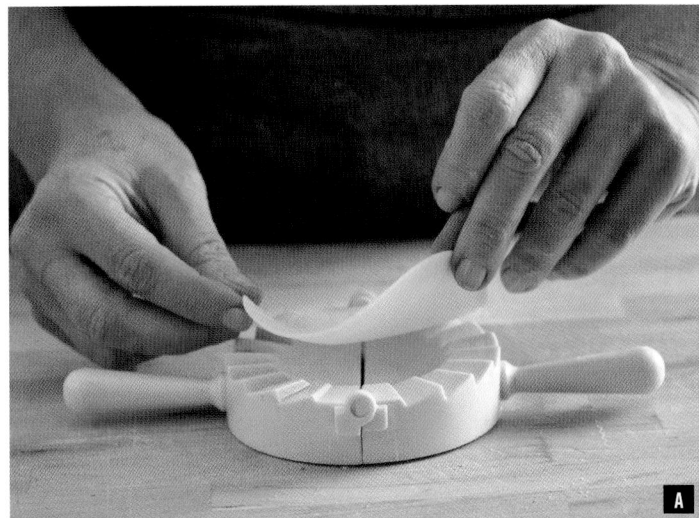
A

B

SOY GINGER DIPPING SAUCE

1 cup (235 ml) Chinese black vinegar (substitute balsamic vinegar)
½ cup (120 ml) soy sauce
½ cup (120 ml) mushroom soy (substitute more soy sauce)
2 tablespoons (16 g) grated fresh ginger
1 teaspoon Korean red pepper flakes (substitute hot red pepper flakes or Chinese chili oil)

Yield: 2 cups (475 ml)

Whisk all together and use as dipping sauce for pot stickers.

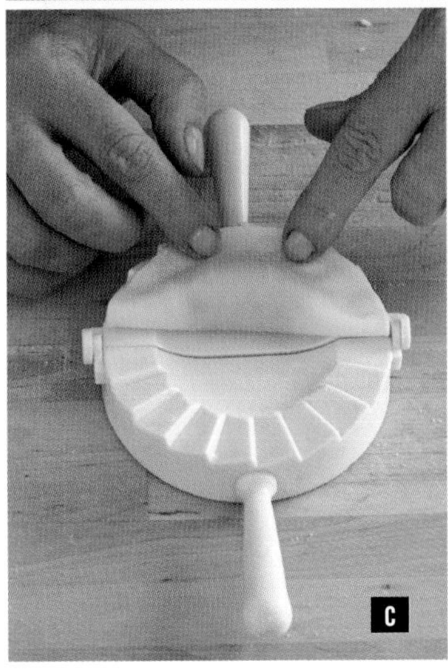
C

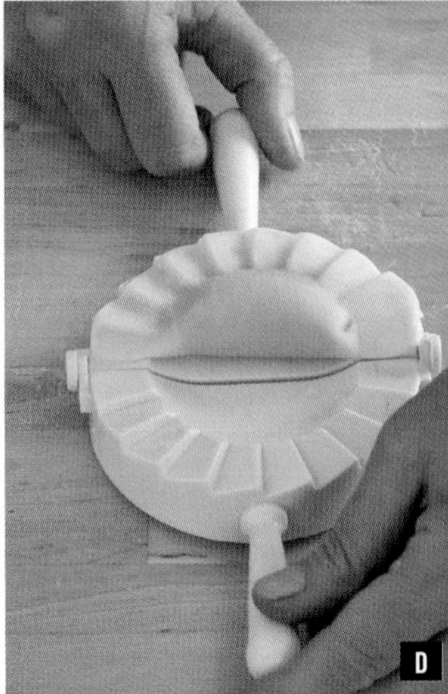
D

UKRAINIAN SOUR CHERRY VARENIKI

SWEET, POACHED, fruit-filled dumplings appear throughout Central Europe. This version from Ukraine is stuffed with sour cherries. Vary the recipe by filling with Italian prune plums or apricots in season. (Cut the fruit in half, remove the pit, stuff with a brandy-soaked sugar cube, cover with the second half, and wrap in dough.)

1 batch Pierogi Dough (page 148)
1 pound (450 g) pitted sour cherries, may be frozen or jarred, drained, and patted dry
16 white or brown sugar cubes
¼ cup (60 ml) brandy
1¼ cups (60 to 75 g) soft white bread crumbs
¼ cup (50 g) sugar
½ teaspoon ground cinnamon
¼ cup (55 g) unsalted butter
½ cup (115 g) sour cream
½ cup (115 g) whole milk plain yogurt

Yield: 16 vareniki, 6 to 8 servings

1. Roll the dough until you can just start to see the grain of wood underneath it, about ⅛-inch (3 mm) thick, or run it through a pasta sheeter to the second-from-last setting.

2. Cut the dough into 4-inch (10-cm) squares **(A)**, rerolling the scraps if desired.

3. Place 6 to 8 well-drained cherries in the centre of the dough square. Dip a cube of sugar in the brandy and place it in the centre of the cherries **(B)**. Brush the edges with water or mist with water from a spray bottle.

4. Pinch together the edges of the dough firmly to seal, trimming off any excess **(C & D)**.

5. Roll each dumpling between the palms of your hands to form it into a round and arrange on a parchment or waxed paper–lined pan, seam-side down **(E)**. Repeat with the remaining cherries, sugar cubes, and dough squares. (Some of the fruit juices may leak, but as long as the vareniki are well-sealed, this is not a problem.)

6 To cook the vareniki, bring a large wide pot of salted water to a boil. Drop the dumplings one by one into the water. Boil gently for about 10 minutes or until the dumplings are puffy and light. Remove with a slotted spoon and drain well on paper or cloth towels. (Once boiled, the dumplings may be tossed with melted butter, wrapped in buttered aluminum foil, and reheated in a 350°F [180°C, or gas mark 4] oven for about 20 minutes.)

7 Meanwhile, in a large skillet, fry the bread crumbs, sugar, and cinnamon in the butter until nicely browned. Roll the dumplings in the bread crumbs, reheating them at the same time if necessary. Whisk together the sour cream and yogurt and serve in a small bowl. Transfer the dumplings to a heated serving dish. Each person spoons the sour cream mixture on their portion.

GENOESE PANSOTTI

PANSOTTI, which means "potbellied," are herb and fresh white cheese–stuffed pasta triangles. In Genoa, they used to be called *gè in preixun* (chard in prison). Today, pansotti are a fixture of Ligurian gastronomy usually served in a creamy walnut and garlic sauce. Pansotti probably originated in Sant'Apollinare, where they were made for the Feast of Saint Joseph, March 19, which always falls during Lent (when meat is not eaten on certain days).

3 bunches assorted tender greens such as watercress, baby arugula, baby spinach, sorrel, or mâche
Green stalks from 1 head fennel
1 bunch scallions, thinly sliced
½ cup (20 g) chopped basil, Italian parsley, or tarragon (or a combination of all 3)
¼ pound (115 g) fresh thick whole milk ricotta cheese
½ cup (25 g) soft bread crumbs
¼ pound (115 g) mixed grated Parmigiano-Reggiano and pecorino Sardo or Romano cheeses
3 large eggs, at room temperature
Fine sea salt, freshly ground black pepper, and freshly ground nutmeg to taste
1 batch Three-Egg Basic Pasta Dough (page 30)
Extra flour for rolling

Yield: 1¾ pounds (800 g), serves 6 to 8

PREPARE THE FILLING:

1 Remove the larger stems from the greens, then wash in a large bowl of cold water, swishing around so sand sinks to the bottom of the bowl. Scoop out the leaves and place in a pot (with a lid) that is large enough to hold them. You should have a total of about 6 cups or 1 pound (450 g) trimmed leaves.

2 Thinly slice the fennel stalks. Place the sliced stalks in a food processor and chop finely. Add the chopped fennel, scallions, and herbs to the pot. Cover and heat on high for 2 to 3 minutes, allowing the greens to wilt in the water that clings to the leaves. Turn once or twice so the greens cook evenly.

3 Drain the greens and run them under cold water to stop the cooking. Squeeze them with your hands to remove most of the liquid, then chop finely.

4 In a large bowl, combine the squeezed greens with the ricotta, bread crumbs, cheeses, eggs, salt, pepper, and nutmeg. Cover and refrigerate until ready to fill the ravioli. If desired, transfer the filling to a disposable pastry bag or a heavy-duty resealable bag and cut out a ½-inch (1-cm) slice from the end or corner. Or, spoon in the filling using a large teaspoon.

ASSEMBLE THE RAVIOLI:

5 Roll out the pasta dough until it is very thin (number 8 on an Atlas machine). Cut each sheet into 2 equal lengths.

6 Emboss the dough with a triangular ravioli maker that measures 3 inches (7.5 cm) on a side **(A)** to use as a guide.

7 Either pipe or spoon about 2 teaspoons of filling evenly spaced about 2 inches (5 cm) apart going down the centre of 1 sheet, taking care not to smear any filling on the edges **(B)**. (The dough will only stick to more dough, not to filling.)

8 Moisten the dough by misting with water from a spray bottle (or brush lightly with water). Cover with the second sheet of dough and press down around the mounds of filling to remove any air **(C)**.

9 Using the triangular ravioli cutter, cut out 1 pansotti with the long edge of the cutter facing down and cut the next one with the long edge facing up, following the embossed markings **(D)**.

10 Remove the trimmings and save to roll out a second time, keeping all the trimmings together in a plastic resealable freezer bag to keep them moist **(E)**. Note that the trimmings will be firmer than the first round because of the flour incorporated while rolling the dough through the sheeter. To compensate for this, have ready a small bowl of cold water to moisten the edges of the pasta before covering with the second sheet.

11 Arrange the filled ravioli on a mesh pasta drying rack, or a clean flour-dusted cotton cloth, turning them after about 30 minutes because this soft, moist filling will begin to make the pansotti stick to the mesh or cloth. Either cook the same day, cover and refrigerate for up to two days, or freeze according to the instructions on page 137.

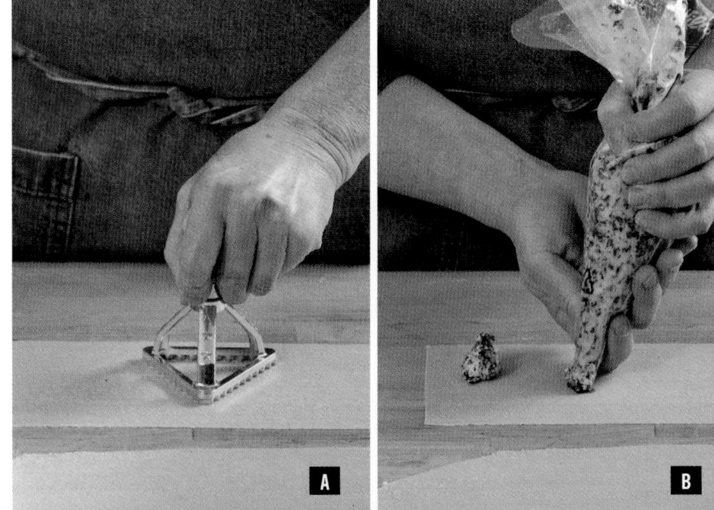

A B

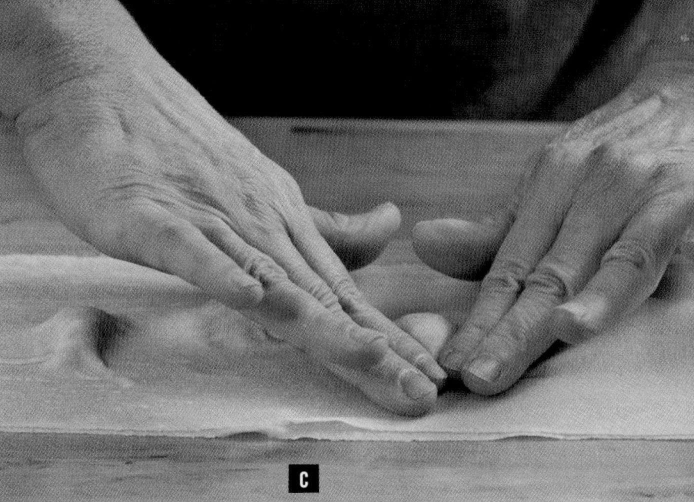

C

D

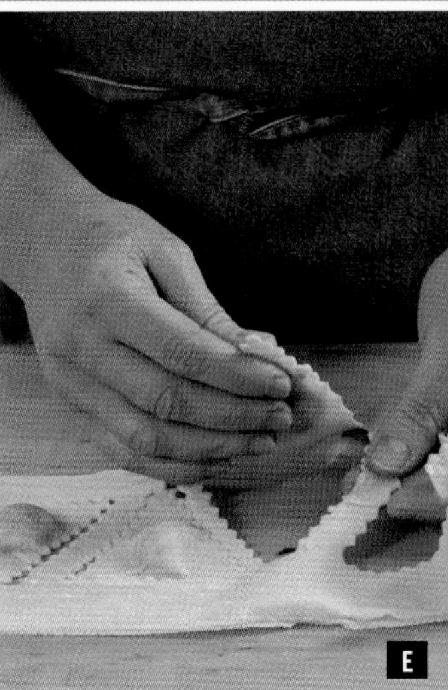

E

GIANT ASPARAGUS RAVIOLO WITH SOFT-COOKED EGG

THIS ARTFUL GIANT raviolo is an impressive dish to serve at a special dinner - one or two per person. It was made famous by the *alta cucina* San Domenico Restaurant in Imola, Italy, in the 1970s and is still on the menu today as "Uovo in Raviolo San Domenico" with a filling of spinach and ricotta, soft-cooked egg, and a truffle-laden butter and Parmigiano sauce. When cutting into the raviolo, the yolk should be liquid and pour out onto the plate, enriching the sauce. Once made, cook and serve the ravioli the same day. Use dense, rich whole milk ricotta for the best results.

1 pound (450 g) thin green asparagus
6 to 8 scallions, trimmed
½ cup (112 g) unsalted butter
2 tablespoons (28 g) unsalted butter
¾ pound (350 g) fresh thick whole milk ricotta cheese
2 ounces (60 g) grated Parmigiano-Reggiano cheese, plus extra for serving
½ cup (25 g) soft white bread crumbs
1 egg yolk
Sea salt, white pepper, and freshly grated nutmeg to taste
12 best-quality fresh-farm eggs, cold (so the yolk won't tend to break open)
1 batch Asparagus Pasta Dough (page 52) or 1 batch Three-Egg Basic Pasta Dough (page 30)
Extra flour for rolling

Yield: 12 ravioli, serves 12 as an appetizer or 6 as a main dish

PREPARE THE FILLING:

1 Trim the white and pale green portions of the asparagus (save the trimmings for vegetable stock if desired). Slice the asparagus thinly. Trim and slice the scallions thinly.

2 Melt the butter in a small skillet. Add the chopped asparagus and scallions and sauté over high heat until the asparagus is brightly coloured and crisp-tender, about 2 minutes. Remove from the heat and cool, then finely chop either by hand or in the bowl of a food processor.

3 Combine the asparagus-scallion mixture with the ricotta, Parmigiano-Reggiano, bread crumbs, and egg yolk in a medium bowl. Mix well, and season to taste with salt, white pepper, and nutmeg. The filling should be firm enough to hold its shape.

4 Transfer the filling to a piping bag or a heavy-duty resealable plastic bag and cut a hole out of one corner about the thickness of a pencil. Reserve. (Filling may be made 1 day ahead, covered, and refrigerated.)

ASSEMBLE THE RAVIOLI:

5 Divide the dough into 4 sections, keeping 3 sections covered. Roll out 1 section to the next-to-thinnest setting on a pasta rolling machine following the directions on page 45. Cut each sheet into 2 equal sections, keeping 1 section covered with plastic wrap to keep it moist.

6 Lightly press a 3¾-inch (9.5-cm) round pastry cutter, preferably scalloped, into the dough sheet to mark out a series of circles **(A & B)**.

7 Carefully pipe a circle of filling about 4⁄10 inch (1 cm) from the edge of the circles, leaving a hole in the centre **(C)**. Take care not to get the filling onto the edge of the dough.

A

B

C

8 Pipe over the first layer of filling in a spiral to create a tower about 2 inches (5 cm) high **(D)**.

9 Carefully break open 1 egg at a time, pouring off most of the white and keeping the yolk whole (it if breaks, save it for another use and use another egg). Pour the yolk and any attached white into the centre of the ricotta ring **(E)**.

10 Cover the filled ravioli with the second sheet of dough **(F & G)**.

11 Drape extra dough around the mounds of filling to accommodate their height **(H)**.

12 Press the dough around the mounds of filling while at the same time pushing out any air pockets, which can cause the finished raviolo to break open **(I)**. Go back over the dough, pressing the sealed edges firmly to ensure they are well-sealed.

13 Cut out individual raviolo with the pastry cutter, pressing the edges well to seal and to thin out the double layer of pasta dough at the edge so it will cook evenly **(J)**. Continue rolling out dough, cutting circles, and filling the ravioli until all dough and filling is used.

Finished giant ravioli **(K)**.

COOK THE GIANT RAVIOLI:

14 Bring a large wide pot of salted water to a boil. Add the ravioli, 1 at a time and no more than 4 in the pot. Bring the water back to the boil, gently releasing the ravioli from the bottom with a silicone spatula or wooden spoon. Once they float, about 2 minutes, boil 1 to 2 minutes longer, or until the edges of the dough are cooked but the centre egg yolk is still liquid.

15 Remove from the pot using a wire skimmer (the ravioli are too fragile to dump into a colander), drain, and serve immediately drizzled with brown butter, grated Parmigiano cheese, and as much truffle as you can bring yourself to use (or use truffle oil). Or sizzle fresh whole sage leaves in the butter before serving.

H
I
J
K

TURKISH MANTI

MANTI ARE dumplings with a meat filling, usually beef or lamb, which originated in Central Asia. Nomads carried manti in frozen or dried form across Central Asia to Anatolia in Turkey, and they were boiled over a campfire. Manti vary in size from substantial to miniature according to region of origin (and cook). Because they are time-consuming to make, preparing manti is a family activity with all ages helping out. Manti can be frozen for up to 1 month.

DOUGH:

½ pound (225 g) unbleached all-purpose flour, plus more for dusting
1 teaspoon sea salt
2 large eggs, at room temperature, lightly beaten
3 to 4 tablespoons (45 to 60 ml) tepid water

FILLING:

2 tablespoons (28 g) unsalted butter
1 small onion, finely diced
½ teaspoon ground cinnamon
Pinch ground cloves
½ pound (225 g) ground lamb (substitute beef)
3 tablespoons (12 g) finely chopped Italian parsley
Sea salt and generous amount of freshly ground black pepper to taste

SAUCES:

4 tablespoons (60 ml) European-style double-concentrated tomato paste or Turkish biber salcasi (sweet–hot red pepper paste)
Sea salt to taste
4 tablespoons (55 g) unsalted butter
2 cups (460 g) thick, strained Greek yogurt
2 or 3 cloves garlic, mashed
Sea salt to taste
2 tablespoons (3.2 g) dried mint, preferably spearmint or ground sumac (or both)
1 tablespoon (3.6 g) Urfa chili flakes (or crushed red pepper flakes)

Yield: about 150 small manti, serves 6 to 8

F

1. Follow the directions in Umbrian Ombrichelli on page 129 to make the dough. Cover the dough with a bowl, a damp kitchen towel, or plastic wrap and allow the dough to rest for 30 minutes at room temperature.

2. Meanwhile, make the filling: Melt the butter until sizzling in a medium skillet. Add the onions, cinnamon, and cloves and cook until the onions are caramelised, about 15 minutes, stirring often. Cool to room temperature.

3. In a medium bowl, combine the lamb, onion mixture, parsley, salt, and pepper. (You may make the filling up to 2 days ahead, cover, and refrigerate.)

4. Roll out 1 portion of the dough lightly dusted with flour on both sides, either using a pasta machine or by hand on a wooden work surface that has been lightly dusted with flour. Roll until the dough is thin enough to see the grain of wood on the work surface, about 1⁄16 inch (2 mm) thick.

5. Cut the sheet of dough into 1¼-inch (3-cm) squares using a knife, rolling square cutter, or a pizza wheel **(A)**.

6 Form small balls of filling, about ½ teaspoon each. Place 1 ball into the centre of a dough square **(B)**.

7 Gently pull 2 opposite corners of dough outward to stretch the dough, then pull together over the filling to meet in the centre, pinching firmly to seal **(C)**.

8 Repeat with remaining 2 corners, pinching to seal while pressing out all the air from the filling pocket **(D)**. This will prevent the manti from opening up while cooking.

9 Twist the points together to seal firmly **(E)**.

10 The filling will show through where it's not covered by the dough. Repeat until all the filling has been used.

11 Arrange the filled manti on parchment or waxed paper–lined baking trays that have been dusted with semolina. Either cook by boiling the same day or freeze following the directions on page 137.

Cooked and drained manti **(F)**.

COOK AND SERVE THE MANTI:

12 To make the sauces, heat the tomato paste, salt, and butter together while whisking to make a smooth sauce. Separately, combine the yogurt, garlic, and salt to make a second sauce.

13 Meanwhile, bring a large pot of salted water to a boil. Add the manti and cook until the filling is firm, 3 to 5 minutes, then drain well. Spoon the manti into serving bowls, topping each with a generous drizzle of the tomato-butter and yogurt sauces. Allow each person to finish the manti to taste with a sprinkle of dried mint or sumac and Urfa chili flakes or crushed red pepper flakes.

A

B

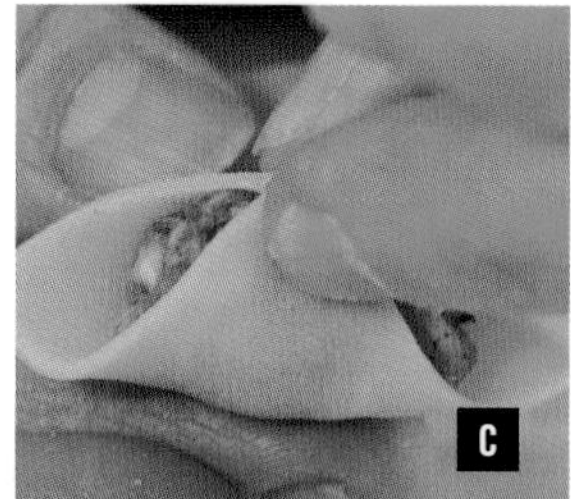
C

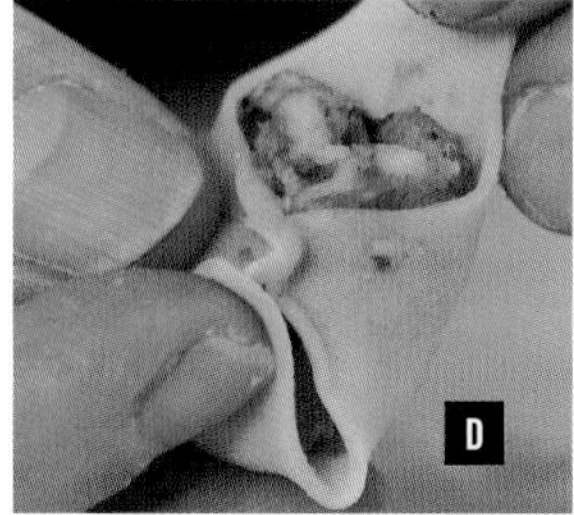
D

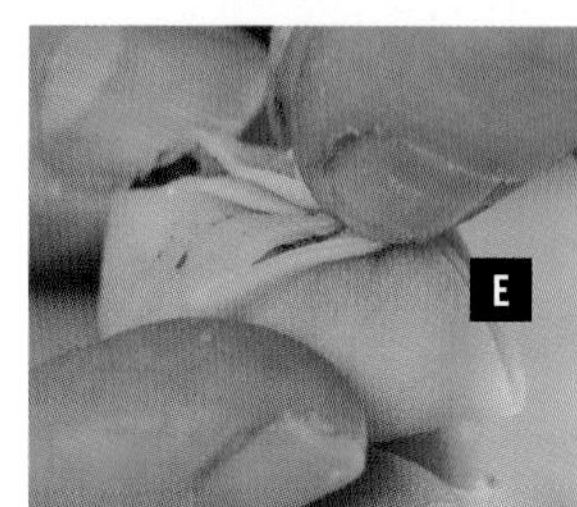
E

SIBERIAN PELMENI

PELMENI ARE meat-filled dumplings that may have originated in Siberia and traveled to China, where they were adapted as pot stickers. It is also possible that pelmeni traveled from China to Siberia, perhaps by the Mongols, along with the black pepper used for seasoning them. Like Central Asian manti, pelmeni were easy to carry and cook during long winter hunting trips and were often kept frozen. The filling is made from uncooked meat (beef, mutton, or pork), wild mushrooms, turnips, or sauerkraut and onions. Pelmeni translates into "ear bread," in yet another ear-shaped pasta. They are boiled or pan-fried (or both) and usually served with melted butter and sour cream, horseradish, tomato sauce, or vinegar. To make them, many cooks use this hexagonal cast-aluminum pelmeni mold.

1 batch Turkish Manti dough (page 162)
1 batch Turkish Manti filling (page 162), made with lamb, or beef, or a combination
Melted butter, sour cream, and vinegar for serving
Extra flour for rolling

Yield: about 150 pelmeni, serves 6 to 8

1 Divide the dough in half, reserving half. Divide one-half in 2 portions and roll each one out on a wooden work surface that has been sprinkled with flour until the dough is very thin and larger by about 2 inches (5 cm) than the diameter of the circular mold. (The dough will be quite soft and stretchy.)

2 Lay 1 dough round over the mold, allowing the excess to drape over the sides **(A)**.

3 Form small balls of filling, about ½ teaspoon each. Place 1 ball into each opening in the pelmeni mold **(B)**. (After placing the filling in the openings, mist the dough with water to moisten if it is dry.)

A

B

4 Drape with a second round of dough **(C)**.

5 Press down with your palms to join the sheets and remove air pockets **(D)**.

6 Roll over the top sheet with a rolling pin, back and forth and from side to side, to join the sheets and cut out the individual pelmeni **(E)**.

7 Turn the form upside down to release the pelmeni **(F)**.

8 Allow the pelmeni to drop from the mold **(G)**.

9 Push out the remaining pelmeni from the mold, one at a time **(H)**. Meanwhile, bring a large pot of salted water to a boil. Carefully drop the pelmeni into boiling water, stirring from time to time to keep them from sticking together. Cook until the filling is firm, 8 to 10 minutes, then drain well. Drizzle with melted butter and serve with small dishes of sour cream and vinegar on the side for dipping. Some people serve ketchup and mayonnaise for dipping the pelmeni.

GLOSSARY

ABRUZZO: Sparsely populated and rather isolated central Italian region. Because it was part of the Kingdom of Two Sicilies, a nineteenth-century union of the Kingdoms of Sicily and Naples, Abruzzo's rustic cuisine is closely connected with the south, and olive oil is the condiment of choice. Specialties include maccheroni or pasta alla chitarra, scrippelle (crepes), lamb, kid, mountain goat, and sheep's milk ricotta.

***ALLA BOSCAIOLA*:** Woodmen's style, an Italian dish involving mushrooms, especially wild mushrooms such as porcini.

***ALTA CUCINA*:** Literally "high cooking," similar to the French *haute cuisine*, a term for the most refined, elegant cooking with an emphasis on beautiful presentations; usually found in top restaurants.

BESCIAMELLA: Cream sauce or white sauce, similar to the French béchamel sauce, today based on milk thickened with a roux (cooked butter and flour paste) but originally made from veal and/or chicken broth. Besciamella is particularly important in the cuisine of Emilia for lasagne, cannelloni, timballo, and other baked pasta.

BIBER SALCASI: Turkish sweet–hot red pepper paste used like tomato paste to season and thicken sauces.

BITTO CHEESE: This DOP cheese is made from whole milk of traditional cow breeds. It is straw-yellow in colour and is made between June 1 and September 30, then aged for a minimum of 70 days. Its name comes from an ancient Celtic word for an Alpine cheese.

BLEACHED FLOUR: Flour is bleached by adding bleach or other chemicals to whiten it and oxidise the surfaces of the flour grains, which helps with developing gluten. Cakes made with bleached flour rise higher using less flour. Those with sensitive palates can detect a slight bitter aftertaste. Unbleached flour is aged naturally over time and is pale yellow to cream in colour.

BRONZE DIES: Extruded pasta dough is forced through a die, traditionally bronze, which forms it into the desired shape. Slightly rough bronze dies make the surface of the pasta jagged and porous, and creamy white, rather than yellow as for pasta extruded through Teflon or other smooth dies. Its textured surface helps hold sauce.

CACIO CHEESE: Sheep's milk cheese that is similar in flavour to Spanish Manchego with a firm, pliable texture and mild flavour that works as a table cheese or for seasoning pasta, especially for *spaghetti al cacio e pepe* (spaghetti with cacio cheese and black pepper).

CAPPELLETTI: Literally "little hats," an alternate name for the stuffed pasta rings known as tortellini in Emilia, used in Le Marche and Umbria, and often made from a square of pasta dough rather than a round.

CASERA CHEESE: This DOP cheese from the Valtellina was first mentioned in dairies in 1500. It is a cylindrical, semi-cooked, and semifat cheese made from the milk of traditional breeds of cow used in traditional regional recipes such as pizzoccheri.

CHINESE BLACK VINEGAR: Inky black aged vinegar made from rice, wheat, millet, sorghum, or a combination with a sweet, complex, malty flavour, which may have sugar, caramel, and spices added. Used for dipping Chinese dumplings.

DOP, IGP: DOP (Denominazione di Origine Protetta, product of protected origin), a program of the European Union to protect the names of regional foods. DOP has highly stringent regulations, and products must come from limited and strictly defined areas. IGP (Indicazione Geografica Protetta, protected geographic indication) products may come from a wider area.

FARMERS' CHEESE: Unripened fresh cheese made by adding bacterial starter and rennet to milk. Once the milk coagulates, the whey is drained off. The cheese is pressed to remove more moisture creating a solid, dry, and crumbly cheese with mild, tangy flavour. It is ideal for filling pierogi and vareniki and is a good substitute for ricotta cheese.

FIDDLEHEAD FERN: These are bright green tightly curled new-growth fronds picked in the wild in their spring season and named for their resemblance to the scroll of a violin head. They taste like slippery asparagus mixed with nutty artichoke.

GRANA PADANO: An Italian DOP cheese named "grana" from the Italian for grain, for its grainy texture, and Padano for the valley where it is made. It was first made about 1,000 years ago by Cistercian monks near Milan. The semifat hard cheese ripens for at least 9 months and is less expensive, though also less complex in flavour than Parmigiano, which must be aged at least 18 months.

GRATIN DISH: A shallow oven-proof dish that is baked or browned under a broiler to give gratin a golden crust.

MARROW: A soft, fatty substance found in the centre of marrow bones, the straight portions of animal leg bones, usually veal and beef. It has the consistency of cold butter and is cream-white in colour streaked lightly with red. It flavours and enriches risotto alla Milanese and Bolognese passatelli.

MARSALA WINE: Wine produced in the region surrounding the Sicilian city of Marsala that is fortified with alcohol, originally so it would last on long ocean voyages, but now for its taste. It is produced in three levels of sweetness: secco (dry), semisecco (semidry), and dolce (sweet). Dry is best for cooking.

MIRIN: Sweet rice wine similar to sake but lower in alcohol and an essential condiment in Japanese cuisine, containing 40 to 50 percent sugar.

MORTADELLA: Smooth-textured, mild-tasting gigantic cooked Italian sausage made of finely ground pork and cubes of pork fat flavoured with black pepper, myrtle, nutmeg, coriander seed, and studded with pistachios. Mortadella originated in Bologna, so its distant American cousin got the name bologna. It is essential to Emilian pasta stuffings, especially tortellini.

NETTLES (OR STINGING NETTLES): *Ortiche* in Italian, a plant with jagged, pointed green leaves and a flavour like spinach. Young leaves are picked and soaked in water or cooked to remove their stinging chemicals. Nettles flavour polenta, pesto, pasta fillings, and dough, especially in Liguria. They are rich in vitamins A and C, iron, and protein.

NORTHERN SWEET POTATOES: Sweet potatoes grown in the northern U.S. with soft cream to yellow flesh and beige skin. They are less sweet and denser than the moist orange sweet potatoes (grown in the southern U.S.), also known as yams. Nancy Hall, Yellow Jersey, and Hayman are three varietals.

OXIDATION: Reaction that occurs when chemicals in food are exposed to oxygen. Plants contain protective antioxidants, but once they are cut or bruised and exposed to air, those defenses are breached. Oxidation of food causes loss of nutritional value and results in discolouration.

PASTA E FAGIOLI: Pasta and beans in Italian, pasta fazool, or pastafazool in southern Italian dialect. Began as a peasant dish made with inexpensive dried beans, such as cannellini and borlotti, and pasta, and may be soupy or thick and stew-like. In winter it often contains cured pork, such as pancetta, and is usually meatless in summer.

RAGÙ: A long-cooked sauce, traditionally served with pasta, made from meat cooked with soffritto (an aromatic mixture of chopped onions, celery, carrots, seasonings), tomatoes, and often wine, then slowly simmered.

RAMPS: Wild leeks that have small white bulbs, rose pink stalks, and broad green leaves. They have a notorious persistent odor like very strong garlic. Ramps are native to eastern North America. The Appalachian name "ramp" comes from the UK, where a related wild plant is known as "ramson."

SANTOKU KNIFE: A Japanese knife that is lighter, thinner, and shorter than a European-style chef's knife and works very well to cut pasta dough strips. Its handle is in line with the top of the blade, curving down to a point. Santoku loosely translates as "three uses" because the knife works well for slicing, dicing, and mincing.

SHISO: Red or green Japanese herb in the basil family, with large ruffle-edged aromatic leaves and a flavour reminiscent of cinnamon, anise, basil, and spearmint, depending on the type. Shiso leaves make an attractive fragrant garnish for noodle soups.

SUMAC: Dried, crushed burgundy-red berries with coarse, moist texture, fruity, tangy flavour, and a salty aftertaste from the salt added as a preservative. It is a popular garnish in the Eastern Mediterranean, sprinkled on salads, manti dumplings, and dips.

TORTELLINO (INCLUDING TORTELLINI, TORTELLI, TORTELLONI): *Torta* is a cake in Italian, and tortellino and tortellini (the plural) are very small "cakes," actually stuffed pasta. Tortelli is an alternate name for ravioli, and tortelloni are similar, large stuffed pasta.

URFA CHILI FLAKES: Also Urfa biber (the Turkish word for pepper), a dried chili cultivated in the Urfa region of Turkey with a smoky, fruity flavour and mild, though long-lasting heat. The peppers ripen from red to dark maroon on the plant.

VACUUM-SEAL: A method of storing food by removing the air to prevent the growth of microorganisms and help prevent evaporation. Vacuum-sealed pasta doughs and fillings keep better and longer and if frozen, don't develop freezer-burn.

RESOURCES

GENERAL RESOURCES

ABOUT EGG SAFETY
www.food.gov.uk/foodindustry/caterers/egg
Egg safety information from the Foods Standard Agency

ABOUT WHEAT FLOUR
www.fabflour.co.uk
Flour information website

DOVES FARM
www.dovesfarm.co.uk
Source for top-quality flours from this UK-based processor and wholesaler of organically grown grains

GLOSSARY OF PASTA SHAPES
www.food-info.net/uk/products/pasta/shapes.htm
Glossary of pasta shapes from Wageningen University, The Netherlands

GUIDETTI FINE FOODS
www.guidetti.co.uk/shop/category/Italian+Flour
Source for imported Italian flours in the UK

INDUSTRIAL PRODUCTION OF PASTA
www.food-info.net/uk/products/pasta/production.htm
About the industrial production of pasta from Wageningen University, The Netherlands

ITALIAN ARTISAN PASTA TOOLS
www.artisanalpastatools.com
Source for hand-carved wooden corzetti molds, garganelli and cavarola boards

L'EPICERIE
www.lepicerie.com
Source for French chestnut flour and French organic specialty flours

MELBURY AND APPLETON
www.melburyandappleton.co.uk
Supplier of specialty flours

MOLINO CAPUTO
www.molinocaputo.it
Website for Molino Caputo, the famed flour mill in Naples, Italy

PAOLO PARISI
www.paoloparisi.it
About Italian goat's milk–fed chickens and their eggs

SAFFRON IN SARDINIA
www.zafferanosargidda.com/saffron.html
About saffron production in Sardinia

SALAMANDER COOKSHOP
www.salamandercookshop.com
Excellent source for pasta tools, including lots of Italian imports, all sizes of pasta cutters, Italian pasta rolling pins, collapsible pasta drying racks, pasta dough knives, pasta sheeters and cutters, and cavatelli makers

SFOGLINE IN BOLOGNA
www.sfogline.it
Video showing Bolognese handmade pasta specialists at work

SFOGLINE CHAMPIONSHIP
www.agriturismo-ridiano.it/lang1/the_sfogline_championship.html
About annual fresh pasta sheet–stretching contest in Italy

WALK MILL FLOUR
www.walkmillflour.co.uk
Source for a variety of wheat flours

WESSEX MILL
www.wessexmill.co.uk
Supplier of a range of culinary flours

BOOKS

BERTOLLI, PAUL. *Cooking by Hand.* New York: Clarkson Potter, 2003.
Bertolli, former chef at Chez Panisse and then Olivetto, and now chef and co-owner of Fra' Mani Handcrafted Salumi, encourages cooks to understand ingredient essentials. He includes a valuable section on evaluating flours for pasta as well as detailed instructions for making different kinds of pasta including spelt, farro, and chestnut flour doughs. Also covered is the process of making, cooking, and saucing pasta.

BRUNO JR., PASQUALE. *Pasta Tecnica.* Contemporary Books, 1985.
Out of print. Although the black and white photography is dated, this remains one of the best books on pasta techniques. Mr. Bruno takes the reader step by step through the use of a manual pasta machine and rolling out pasta by hand, as well as illustrating various methods of forming ravioli, gnocchi, tortellini, and other classics.

BUGIALLI, GIULIANO. *Bugialli on Pasta.* New York: Stewart, Tabori & Chang, 2000.
The master at work in this classic includes excellent detailed line drawings of pasta techniques plus many recipes with photographs showing traditional pasta and the tools used to create them.

CALLEN, ANNA TERESA. *Food and Memories of Abruzzo: Italy's Pastoral Land.* Hoboken, NJ: Wiley, 2004.
Author and cooking teacher Anna Teresa Callen grew up in Abruzzo and presents its rustic, vibrant regional specialties in this book, along with her childhood memories of rolling out pasta by hand with her mother. The book features more than 350 traditional Abruzzese recipes including the region's famed *pasta alla chitarra* (guitar-cut fresh pasta).

CASELLA, CESARE. *True Tuscan: Flavors and Memories from the Countryside of Tuscany.* New York: William Morrow Cookbooks, 2005.
As a fellow bean-lover, I immediately hit it off with Cesare Casella, renowned Tuscan chef working in New York and author of the Foreword for this book, the first time we met. Here, Casella shares the rustic Tuscan cooking that he grew up with including fresh pasta, such as mushroom lasagna, lasagna with black-eyed peas, artichoke ravioli, and *ravioli di pesce* (fish-stuffed ravioli). Casella's food is quite delicious, without pretension, bold, rustic, and full of flavour.

GHEDINI, FRANCESCO. *Northern Italian Cooking.* New York: Plume Books, 1984.
A small, unassuming, out-of-print book, this is a very personal collection of

traditional recipes from Northern Italy. Ghedini's work is charming, his recipes work beautifully, and his flavours are bold and simple. Ahead of its time.

GOSETTI DELLA SALDA, ANNA. *Le Ricette Regionale Italiane.* Milan: Casa Editrice Solares, 1st edition 1967, 16th edition 2005.
My dog-eared, go-to book for authentic regional Italian food since I carried my first copy home from Italy in 1979, complete with charming drawings of traditional tools and ingredients plus original dialect names for the dishes. I met with the late author many years ago, as I wanted to translate this incredibly valuable book, though that project never came to fruition.

HAZAN, MARCELLA. *Essentials of Classic Italian Cooking.* New York: Alfred A. Knopf, 1992.
Hazan's influence on Italian cooking, especially in the United States, is enormous. This book, which combines the best of her first two books (*The Classic Italian Cookbook* and *More Classic Italian Cooking*) with new material, is the ultimate source, especially for the lavish cooking of Emilia-Romagna.

ILKIN, NUR, AND SHEILAH KAUFMAN. *The Turkish Cookbook: Regional Recipes and Stories.* Northampton, MA: Interlink Books, 2010.
Sheilah Kaufman, working with her Turkish colleague Nur Ilkin, who learned to cook from her grandmother, produced a beautiful cookbook about the earthy regional foods of Turkey from the Mediterranean and Aegean Coasts to the Black Sea region and the far reaches of Eastern Turkey. (I wrote the Foreword.) See the trahana soup and simple pasta with cheese and walnuts.

KREMEZI, AGLAIA. *The Foods of the Greek Islands: Cooking and Culture at the Crossroads of the Mediterranean.* New York: Houghton Mifflin, 2000.
Aglaia Kremezi, Greek culinary journalist and author, has written a collection of books about the food of her native Greece. In this lavishly photographed large-scale book, Kremezi offers her informed and authentic recipes for the deliciously varied cuisine of the Greek Islands, including trahana (dried yogurt-vegetable-semolina dough bits) from the large island of Chios.

MACHLIN, EDDA SERVI. *The Classic Cuisine of the Italian Jews: Traditional Recipes and Menus and a Memoir of a Vanished Way of Life.* New York: Dodd, Mead & Co., 1981.
This classic book brings together two of my personal obsessions: Italian cooking and the world of Jewish food.

RE, GIANNA, ED. *La Cucina Italiana: Grandi Vini e Ricette della Regioni Italiane.* Casale Monferrato: Edizione Piemme Spa, 2005.
926 pages of Italian food and wines (in Italian) by region and by subject with lots of appetizing photo inserts. Good source for wine pairing ideas. The recipes are written in Italian style using metric measurements and with measurements given only for major ingredients and assuming basic culinary knowledge.

SERVENTI, SILVANO, AND FRANÇOISE SABBAN. *Pasta: The Story of a Universal Food.* New York: Columbia University Press, 2002.
A thorough, well-researched history of Italian pasta from the stuffed pastas of the Middle Ages to the earliest industrial pastas to today's artisan pasta revival and modern industrial pasta. A section on pasta in China begins in ancient times, leads up through the Ming Dynasty, to modern-day ramen noodles.

WECHSBERG, JOSEPH. *The Cooking of Vienna's Empire* (Foods of the World Series). New York: Time-Life Books, 1968.
When I first started cooking professionally, I depended on the incredibly well-researched, detailed recipes and background articles in this series for my catering business. A friend had a subscription and I waited anxiously every month for a new book to arrive. Only years later was I able to afford to buy them for myself. Forty years later, their value is lasting, and the recipes have authentic flavour.

ZANINI DE VITA, ORETTA. *Encyclopedia of Pasta (California Studies in Food and Culture).* Berkeley, CA: University of California Press, 2009.
A fascinating, well-organised book that illustrates traditional Italian pasta in its myriad forms, extravagant shapes, and colourful dialect names. Food scholar Oretta Zanini De Vita traveled to every corner of Italy to record oral histories, delve into family cookbooks, and search archives to produce this valuable and engaging book.

Use this table if you do not have a kitchen scale and you would like to convert the recipes from weights into volume measures. (The metric measurements provided in the recipes are used for measuring ingredients by weight and are not included in this chart.)

FLOUR AND GRAIN WEIGHT AND VOLUME EQUIVALENTS

Weight	Volume
ALL-PURPOSE FLOUR, UNBLEACHED	
¼ pound all-purpose flour	1 cup minus 1 tablespoon
½ pound all-purpose flour	2 cups minus 2 tablespoons
¾ pound all-purpose flour	3 cups minus 3 tablespoons
1 pound all-purpose flour	3¾ cups
BARLEY FLOUR	
¼ pound barley flour	¾ cup plus 2 tablespoons
6 ounces barley flour	1¼ cups plus 1 tablespoon
½ pound barley flour	1¾ cups
1 pound barley flour	3½ cups
BUCKWHEAT FLOUR	
¼ pound buckwheat flour	1 cup minus 1 tablespoon
½ pound buckwheat flour	2 cups minus 2 tablespoons
BREAD FLOUR (UNBLEACHED)	
¼ pound bread flour	1 cup
½ pound bread flour	2 cups
1 pound bread flour	4 cups
CHESTNUT FLOUR	
2 ounces chestnut flour	½ cup minus ½ tablespoon
3 ounces chestnut flour	¾ cup minus 1 tablespoon
¼ pound chestnut flour	1 cup minus 1 tablespoon
6 ounces chestnut flour	1½ cups minus 2 tablespoons
CHICKPEA FLOUR	
3 ounces	1 cup
6 ounces	2 cups
¾ pound	4 cups

Weight	Volume
CORNMEAL, STONE-GROUND	
¼ pound cornmeal	¾ cup plus 2 tablespoons
½ pound cornmeal	1¾ cups
1 pound cornmeal	3½ cups
DURUM WHEAT FLOUR	
¼ pound durum wheat flour	¾ cup plus 2 tablespoons
½ pound durum wheat flour	1¾ cups
1 pound durum wheat flour	3½ cups
PASTA FLOUR MIX	
¼ pound Pasta Flour Mix	1¼ cups
½ pound Pasta Flour Mix	2½ cups
¾ pound Pasta Flour Mix	3¾ cups
1 pound Pasta Flour Mix	5 cups
RYE FLOUR (DARK)	
¼ pound dark rye flour	1 cup minus 2 tablespoons
½ pound dark rye flour	1¾ cups
1 pound dark rye flour	3½ cups
SEMOLINA, FINE	
¼ pound fine semolina	½ cup plus 2½ tablespoons
6 ounces fine semolina	1 cup
½ pound fine semolina	1¼ cups plus 1 tablespoon
1 pound fine semolina	2½ cups plus 2 tablespoons
WHOLE WHEAT FLOUR	
¼ pound whole wheat flour	1 cup
6 ounces whole wheat flour	2 cups
½ pound whole wheat flour	3 cups
1 pound whole wheat flour	4 cups

INDEX

ACKNOWLEDGMENTS

My heartfelt thanks to everyone who helped me learn more about pasta, especially my host in Orvieto, Velia de Angelis, of Velia's Cooking Style and La Champagneria, and Valentina Santanicchio, chef/proprietor of Al Saltapicchio, also in Orvieto. These two chefs were my excellent tutors in hand-rolling pasta and Umbrian ombrichelli, and they generously shared the techniques and tips they learned at the youngest age from their own mothers and grandmothers.

Fond memories and many thanks go to Maya Eisner and Claudio Roncoroni, of Residence Ramerino e Agriturismo Leccino, who showed me their Maremma and arranged for me to visit Pastificio Caponi near Pisa. *Grazie* also to Andrea and Alessandro Tagliagambe, the two brothers who run Caponi. They invited me to tour their small (five-person) artisanal pasta factory where they make no more than 170 kilos (375 pounds) of fresh egg pasta daily. The company credits the hard mineral-rich water, fresh local eggs, durum semolina, and more than fifty years of know-how for its outstanding quality.

Grazie to Patrizia and Doriana Schiazo, two sisters who welcomed my hovering over them in the small shop in Orvieto where they hand-roll their *Pasta Fresca, Lavorazione a Mano* (fresh pasta, handmade) daily. Mariella Giovannucci, owner, and Nadia Vesci, buyer, of Fante's Kitchen Wares Shop, generously shared their extensive knowledge of the best pasta tools. Nadia, who personally tested every one of the tools I used in this book, was able to answer all my questions. It's always a thrill to walk into Fante's faced with the difficult task of deciding just what perfectly designed kitchen tools and toys I need for my latest project.

Betty Kaplan (of Culinary Confidence) was my peerless, careful, and caring assistant as we tested the recipes and techniques time and again. No matter how many dozens of eggs I bought, we were sure to run out by the end of the day! Making batch after batch of pasta dough, we worked hard and developed our upper body strength, but we always had fun and laughed a lot. Two culinary pros, Adrienne Abramson (of the Artful Chef) and Linda Gellman, also came to work with me, practicing, testing and, of course, sampling some great pasta.

Many thanks to Clare Pelino, of ProLiterary Consultants, who made the happy match between me and Quarry Books. Thanks to Steve Legato, whose love of food is apparent in his carefully composed photographs. He tells a good bawdy joke, and he really appreciates great pasta. This is the ninth book we've worked on together, and I hope one of many more to come. A special shout-out to Rochelle Bourgault, a talented editor who is not only excellent at her job, but also has a great sense of humor.

- ALIZA GREEN

ABOUT THE AUTHOR AND PHOTOGRAPHER

ABOUT THE AUTHOR

ALIZA GREEN, author, consultant, and influential chef, has been a pasta fanatic ever since she spent a summer in Italy at age six. She studied with Marcella Hazan, from whom she learned to make fresh pasta for the Bolognese-inspired Ristorante DiLullo, where she served as Executive Chef. She studied Italian to read cookbooks and culinary publications in their original language, and to meet and work with chefs and food producers in Italy. With the help of the restaurant's three resident pasta artisans, Green prepared enough fresh pasta to serve hundreds of customers daily, all cooked to order - a formidable task in a restaurant that seated more than 200. As chef, consultant, and teacher, she continued to develop her pasta skills and broaden her repertoire of imaginative fresh homemade pasta.

Green is the James Beard Award–winning author of ten successful food guides and cookbooks on subjects ranging from beans, fish, and baking to produce, herbs and spices, and meat. She now leads culinary tours of Italy, especially in the Tuscan Maremma and Umbria, working with Epicopia, a leader in the field.

WWW.ALIZAGREEN.COM

ABOUT THE PHOTOGRAPHER

STEVE LEGATO's passion for photography has granted him the humbling opportunity to work with some of the most dedicated, passionate, and creative chefs you've heard of and dozens you haven't heard of - yet. His photography has been featured in *Art Culinaire*, the *New York Times*, *Bon Appetit*, *GQ*, *Wine Spectator*, *Food Arts*, *Travel + Leisure*, and *Wine & Spirits*. He has photographed more than thirty cookbooks, including *!Ceviche!* (co-written by Aliza Green), which won a James Beard Award in 2002, and *Restaurant Nicholas: The Cookbook*, which was nominated for the 2010 International Association of Culinary Professionals Cookbook award for photography. He has been known to drive through the night for a perfect bowl of tagliatelli with porcini.

WWW.STEVELEGATO.COM